LA PÂTISSERIE DES RÊVES

THE PÂTISSERIE OF DREAMS

Grub Street · London

This English language edition published in 2014 by
Grub Street
4 Rainham Close
London
SW11 6SS
Email: food@grubstreet.co.uk
Web: www.grubstreet.co.uk

Copyright this English language edition © Grub Street 2014
Translation: Tamsin Black
Copyright original French edition © Éditions Gründ, 2012
Photographs © Nicolas Mathéus
Photographs pages 43, 44, 45 © Julien Bourrély; page 65 © Franck Beloncle; pages 18, 47, 66, 220, 221, 227 © Yves Duronsoy
Artistic director: Thierry Teyssier
Editorial director: Karine Bailly
Publisher: Marine Schoeser
Editor: Thierry Roussillon
Cover graphic design: Krista Sochor
Layout: Elise Bonhomme and Patrick Leleux PAO
A CIP catalogue record for this book is available from the British Library

ISBN 978-1-909808-17-1

Printed and bound in Slovenia

PHILIPPE CONTICINI   THIERRY TEYSSIER

Photography by Nicolas Mathéus

LA PÂTISSERIE DES RÊVES

THE PÂTISSERIE OF DREAMS

CONTENTS

VIENNOISERIES

Light Kouign-amann	page 24
Gourmet Pains au Chocolat	page 26
Chaussons Napolitains	page 28
Brioche Mousseline	page 30
Croissants	page 32
Tangy Windmills	page 34
Vanilla and Bergamot Follies	page 36
Vanilla and Sultana Briochins	page 38
Apple and Honey Spread	page 40

TEATIME TREATS

Marbled Chocolate and Hazelnut Cake	page 48
Vanilla Flan	page 50
Chocolate Sponge Cake	page 52
Dreamy Madeleines	page 54
Coconut, Ginger and Crunchy Sugar Cake	page 56
Conversation…Lemon and Hazelnut	page 58
Bittersweet Orange Cake	page 60
Gâteaux Bretons with Brown Sugar	page 62

SALON DE THÉ

Creamed Rice	page 68
Floating Islands, Vanilla and Praline	page 70
Crème Caramel	page 72
Brown Sugar Waffles	page 74
Chocolate Mousse	page 76
White Chocolate Lava Cakes with Lemon	page 78
Citrus Salad with a Tangy Jus	page 80
Semolina Cake	page 82
Fruit Tagine	page 84

BISCUITS

Spicy Almond and Fruit Fondant Biscuits	page 90
Caramel and Crystallised Ginger Tuiles	page 92
Praline Shortbread	page 94
Soft Cantuccini	page 96
Langues de Chat with Green Tea and White Chocolate	page 98
Spicy Banana Tuiles with Black Sesame Seeds	page 100
Tasty Shortbread	page 102
Coconut Snaps	page 104
Ladyfingers with Matcha Tea	page 106

THE CLASSICS

Saint-Honoré	page 112
Religious Dreams	page 114
Tarte Tatin	page 116
Paris-Brest	page 118
Rum Babas	page 120
Chocolate Gâteau	page 122
Salambos	page 124
Cherry Clafoutis	page 126

SEASONAL FRUIT TARTS

Rhubarb Tart	*page 132*
Tangy Strawberry Tart	*page 134*
Apple Tartlets	*page 136*
Quince Tarte Tatin	*page 138*
Mango and Pineapple Tart	*page 140*
Pear Tart with Champomy® Caramel	*page 142*
Orange Tart	*page 144*
Banana and Coffee Tart	*page 146*
Blueberry and Almond Tart	*page 148*

FREESTYLE CAKES

Sugared Almond Cake	*page 154*
Snow Meringues	*page 156*
Goats Cheese Tart with Mango and Avocado	*page 158*
Coffee Cake	*page 160*
Raspberry and Matcha Tea Cake	*page 162*
Lemon Cream Choux Buns	*page 164*
Rich Coffee Log	*page 166*

CONFECTIONERY

Praline Paste	*page 172*
Rhubarb Paste	*page 174*
Caramels with Salted Butter	*page 176*
Vanilla Crème Pâtissière	*page 178*
Hazelnut and Fleur de Sel Streusel	*page 180*
Sweet Chocolate Ice Cream	*page 182*
Nougat	*page 184*
Red Fruit Compote	*page 186*
Marbled Praline Ice Cream	*page 188*
Citrus Fruit Jellies	*page 190*

LESSONS ON TASTE

Products	*page 197*
Basic recipes step by step	*page 207*
Pâte Sucrée	*page 208*
Inverse Puff Pastry in the electric mixer	*page 209*
Sweet Choux Pastry in the electric mixer	*page 210*
Vanilla Crème Pâtissière	*page 211*
Hazelnut and Fleur de Sel Streusel	*page 212*
Fruit Tagine	*page 213*
French Flan Pastry (pâte à foncer) in the electric mixer	*page 214*
Caramalised Ground Mixed Nuts	*page 215*
Crème Pralinée	*page 216*
Crème Anglaise	*page 217*
Philippe's Tips	*page 219*

INDEX   *page 228*

PREFACE

La Pâtisserie des Rêves was the fruit of our meeting and our
friendship.

The starting point was our mutual creativity and a strong urge to
express our feelings and let the big kid in us speak out.

When we opened La Pâtisserie des Rêves, our aim was simple but
ambitious: we wanted to appeal to young and old by offering them
great classic cakes of mouth-watering French pâtisserie – cakes
which give today's children the same pleasure that forged the
sensory and emotional memory in ourselves, the grown-up children
we still are.

What could be more wonderful than to conjure up magical
moments when young and old come together! You, Thierry,
expressed that magic in your marvellous décor of transparent domes
on round and oval tables – a tribute to the carousels of miniature
horses you rode in your childhood. Those ingenious displays were
your idea to showcase my cakes as you wished.

As for you, Philippe, your sensitivities found expression in delicious
cakes, which captivated me before beguiling everybody else. Ah,
your Paris-Brest and Tarte Tatin, your Saint-Honoré… the list is
endless!

To cut a long story short, this book is an attempt to bring you the magic of La Pâtisserie des Rêves and rekindle the delight we feel every day of the week (including Sunday) as we watch your eyes sparkle.

Magical flavours in a magical universe. Take it from us: every chapter will open doors into a whole world of lusciousness you will never want to leave. Viennoiseries, biscuits, classics or freestyle pastries – you'll find them irresistible!

The recipes all provide full details to help you reproduce at home the creations you can find in our pastry shops, and above all, to help you recapture the pleasure of eating them. But before you get started, we'll tell you the secret that has informed our way of working for years: 'put what you are into what you do'.

Now, over to you to play and 'pâtisser'. Roll up your sleeves, don't be afraid to get your hands dirty, and above all, be sure to try everything you make: you won't be disappointed!

Philippe Conticini
Thierry Teyssier

LA PÂTISSERIE DES RÊVES
PAR PHILIPPE CONTICINI

VIENNOISERIES

Light Kouign-amann

*For 12 Kouign-amanns
(depending on their size)*
Preparation: 1hr 50mins
Resting time: 9hours
Cooking time: 20mins

400g flour
   (+ for the work surface)
12g table salt
340g unsalted butter
   (+ a little for the baking tray)
8g fresh yeast
20ml water
200g granulated sugar

FOR THE DOUGH

Tip the flour, salt and 15g of butter cut into chunks into the bowl of an electric mixer. Combine everything with the dough hook at low speed for 2 minutes, then immediately tip in the yeast first dissolved in 100 ml of cold water. Add the remaining water.

ALLOW THE DOUGH TO RISE

Continue kneading on medium speed for another 5 minutes until the dough is smooth and homogenous. Leave the dough in the bowl, then cover it with cling film and allow to rise at room temperature for one and a half hours until doubled in size.

PUT THE DOUGH IN THE FRIDGE

Turn the dough out on to the floured work surface and flip it over two or three times with your hand from bottom to top to return it to its original ball-shape. Then put it on a sheet of baking parchment, cover with cling film and refrigerate for 2 hours.

ROLL OUT THE BUTTER

Place the remaining butter (which should be very soft) between 2 sheets of baking parchment and pound it with the rolling pin then roll it out into a rectangle about 20 x 25cm to a thickness of 5mm to 1cm. Put the butter in the fridge for about an hour and a half. Butter and dough should be the same temperature.

GIVE THE DOUGH THE FIRST TWO TURNS

Now roll out the dough on the floured work surface to make a rectangle about 45 x 25cm. Place the rectangle of butter in the middle of the dough and fold the flaps of dough into the centre of the butter so the edges meet. Roll it all out to obtain a strip about 70cm long. Fold the dough again, this time into three layers like a folding wallet. Give the dough a quarter turn then roll it out to obtain another 70cm-long strip. Now, give it a second turn exactly like the first one. Wrap it up in cling film then let the dough rest in the fridge for one and a half hours.

TO FINISH THE DOUGH

Give the dough another two turns but this time, sprinkle it with sugar before folding it into the wallet-shape to fully incorporate it. Wrap the dough in cling film again then put it in the fridge for at least an hour.

SHAPE THE KOUIGN-AMANN

Roll out the dough into a 40 x 90cm rectangle. Sprinkle the dough with sugar before every roll. Cut the dough into squares with 10cm sides then fold the corners into the centre. Dip the kouign-amanns in the sugar to give them a good coating then lay them on a well-buttered baking tray sprinkled with the remaining sugar. Allow to rest at room temperature (between 22°C and 24°C) for one and a half hours.

TO COOK

Preheat the oven to 170°C (gas mark 3 to 4). Bake the kouign-amanns for about 20 minutes until crisp and a deep golden colour on the outside but melting on the inside. Allow to cool before serving.

Gourmet Pains au Chocolat

For 6 pains au chocolat
Preparation: 40mins
Resting time: 3hours
Cooking time: 45mins

75g dark chocolate
50g unsalted butter
20ml water
2 level tablespoons milk
    powder (12g)
25g yeast
395g type 55 flour
    (+ for the work surface)
40g brown sugar
40g thick cream
1 level tablespoon fleur de sel
2 tablespoons cocoa powder (10g)
60g dark chocolate chips

TO FINISH
1 egg
brown sugar

KNEAD THE DOUGH IN THE MIXER

Chop up the butter and chocolate and melt the pieces in a bain-marie.

Dissolve the milk powder in water, warm the milk then pour it together with the yeast into the bowl of an electric mixer fitted with a dough hook. Add the flour, brown sugar, cocoa powder, fleur de sel and thick cream. Set the mixer going at low speed for 5 minutes to start kneading then increase the speed to medium. Count 5 minutes before switching back to low speed to mix in the warm melted chocolate and butter, a third at a time. When the dough starts to come away from the sides of the bowl, tip in the chocolate chips.

SHAPE THE PAINS AU CHOCOLAT

Place the dough on the floured work surface then cut it into 6 rolls weighing 150g each. Roll them into balls between floured hands. Lay the balls on a tray lined with a sheet of baking parchment then allow to 'grow' at room temperature (22°C to 24°C) for 3 hours until doubled in size.

GLAZE THE PAINS AU CHOCOLAT

Preheat the oven to 170°C (gas mark 3 to 4). Brush the pastries with beaten egg then sprinkle liberally with brown sugar. Put them in the oven for about 35 to 40 minutes. Allow to cool before serving.

Chaussons Napolitains

For around 15 chaussons
Preparation time: 1hour
Freezing time: 40mins
Refrigeration time: 1hour
Cooking time: 30mins

70g brown sugar

2 teaspoons vanilla essence

Zest of 1 orange

Zest of 1 lemon

50g macadamia nuts

200g puff pastry (see page 209)

1 egg to glaze

Icing sugar

FOR THE RAISINS

50g raisins

3 tablespoons rum

1 teaspoon brown sugar

FOR THE SWEETENED BUTTER

60g butter

15g brown sugar

FOR THE CRÈME PÂTISSIÈRE

100ml semi-skimmed milk

1 egg yolk

15g caster sugar

10g type 55 flour

5g cold butter

30ml rum

1 vanilla pod

FOR THE CHOUX PASTE

45ml water / 45ml rum

90ml semi-skimmed milk

70g butter / 90g flour

140g whole eggs (3 eggs)

1 teaspoon caster sugar

1 level teaspoon table salt

FOR THE RAISINS WITH RUM

Marinate the raisins in the rum and sugar mixture. Set aside.

FOR THE SWEETENED BUTTER

Mix together the brown sugar and very soft creamed butter. Beat vigorously for 20 seconds.

FOR THE CRÈME PÂTISSIÈRE

In a saucepan, bring the milk and vanilla pod to the boil.

Meanwhile, whisk the egg yolk and sugar thoroughly then add the flour. Off the heat, remove the vanilla pod from the milk and pour the boiling vanilla milk over the previous mixture in two or three batches, continuing to whisk vigorously. Transfer everything to the pan and bring the mixture back to the boil, but gently and slowly over a medium heat and don't stop whisking. Cook the cream for 1 minute, still whisking to prevent it sticking to the bottom of the pan. When the cream has thickened up, still on the heat, vigorously whisk in the cold butter then the rum. Pour the still-hot cream into a mixing bowl and pat cling film down over the surface to prevent a crust forming. Place in the fridge.

FOR THE CHOUX PASTRY

Cut the butter into chunks. Pour the milk and water into a saucepan followed by the pieces of butter.

Bring to the boil then add the sifted dry ingredients (flour, salt and sugar) in one go. Stir carefully: a dough will form immediately. Continue stirring over a medium heat for 1 minute to eliminate as much moisture as possible. Now tip the dough into the bowl of an electric mixer and knead it with the paddle (the flat beater attachment), incorporating the whole eggs one at

a time. You should obtain a pliable, glossy dough. To check whether it is ready, drag your finger quite deeply over the surface for a few centimetres: the groove should gently close up afterwards. Whisk the crème pâtissière vigorously into the choux paste, followed by the brown sugar, vanilla extract, the zests, crushed macadamia nuts and the rum-marinated raisins.

TO ASSEMBLE THE CHAUSSONS

Roll out the puff pastry to 1.5mm thick, cut it into a 30 x 60cm rectangle then spread a thin layer of the sweetened butter over it, leaving a 1cm edge. Roll up the dough tightly to make an even sausage shape.

Wrap in cling film and place in the freezer for at least 40 minutes.

When the sausage is firm but not yet frozen, cut it into slices ½cm thick. Pass the rolling pin over the slices to make them slightly oval (but not too long) and line them up in front of you.

On the lower half of each slice, place a generous mound of choux paste, leaving a 2cm edge.

Fold the puff pastry over the choux paste but make sure you leave the chausson open.

Brush the chaussons with beaten egg then put the filled chaussons in the fridge for 1 hour.

TO BAKE

Bake the chaussons in the oven at 170°C (gas mark 3 to 4) for 30 minutes.

When they are done, sprinkle with icing sugar. Serve warm or at room temperature, but definitely not hot.

Brioche Mousseline

For 6 to 8 people
Preparation time: 45mins
Resting time: 7hours
Cooking time: 35mins

250g flour (+ for the work
   surface)
40g caster sugar
1 level teaspoon salt (6g)
10g fresh yeast
4 chilled eggs
190g butter at room temperature

MAKE THE DOUGH IN THE ELECTRIC MIXER
Take the butter out of the fridge 30 minutes before starting the recipe. Break the chilled eggs into a mixing bowl. Stir and dissolve the yeast in them. Tip the flour, salt and sugar into the bowl of an electric mixer fitted with a dough hook. Set the mixer going, adding the mixture of eggs and yeast. Knead at low speed in short bursts for the dough to form. When the mixture has fully bound together, set the mixer to a medium speed for 7 to 8 minutes until the dough comes away from the sides.

INCORPORATE THE BUTTER
Now, cut up the butter into small chunks and tip the pieces into the mixer bowl. Continue kneading for about 3 to 4 minutes until the dough comes away from the sides again and is a smooth, homogenous consistency.

ALLOW THE DOUGH TO REST
Take the bowl out of the mixer. Leave the dough in the bowl and cover with cling film so that the film is touching the dough. Allow to rise at room temperature for about one and a half hours until it has more-or-less doubled in size.

PUT THE DOUGH IN THE FRIDGE
Take out the dough, place it on the floured work surface and flip it over two or three times with your hand from bottom to top to return it to its initial ball shape. Now place it on a sheet of baking parchment, cover with cling film and refrigerate for 3 hours.

CUT THE DOUGH INTO PIECES
Flour the dough and roll it into a sausage shape 16cm long. Cut the sausage into 4 equal pieces then put them into an 18 to 20cm long Teflon® loaf tin. Cover the tin with cling film then leave the balls to rise at room temperature for 2 hours until they are 75% bigger.

TO BAKE
Preheat the oven to 170°C (gas mark 3 to 4). Place the brioches on a baking tray lined with baking parchment and bake in the oven for about 35 minutes.

Croissants

For about 15 croissants
Preparation time: 2hours 10mins
Resting time: 10hours 30mins
Cooking time: 12mins

340g flour (type 45, if possible)

10g fresh yeast

335g butter, at room temperature

8g table salt

55g caster sugar

40ml water

40ml semi-skimmed milk

1 whole egg

FOR THE LEAVEN

90g flour

20g fresh yeast

80ml semi-skimmed milk

FOR THE LEAVEN

Crumble the yeast into a mixing bowl and combine it with the flour. Whisk in the milk to form a smooth, homogenous dough. Cover the bowl with cling film and leave the mixture to rise at room temperature for about one to one and a half hours.

FOR THE CROISSANT DOUGH

Crumble the yeast into the bowl of an electric mixer then pour the lightly warmed milk and water over it. Cover with the flour, salt, sugar and 85g melted but cold butter then add the leaven. Mix everything with the dough hook on low speed to obtain a homogenous dough then continue kneading on medium speed for 5 minutes to allow the gluten in the flour to form into an elastic network. Leave the dough in the bowl and cover with cling film. Allow the dough to rise at room temperature for one and a half hours until more-or-less doubled in size. Knead the dough by hand to return it to its initial shape. Wrap it in cling film then refrigerate for about 2 hours.

ROLL OUT THE BUTTER

Place the remaining butter between 2 sheets of baking parchment and pound it with the rolling pin then roll it out into a square with 15cm sides to 1cm thick. Place this square of butter in the fridge.

FOR THE PUFF PASTRY

Roll out the dough into a rectangle 60cm long by 20cm wide. Lay the butter in the middle of the dough and fold the ends of the dough into the centre so that they overlap.

TURNING THE DOUGH

Roll out the dough into a 60 x 20cm rectangle. Fold this strip into three overlapping sections like a wallet. Give the dough a quarter turn then wrap it in cling film and allow to rest in the fridge for at least an hour. Repeat the process twice more, making sure you let it rest in the fridge wrapped in cling film for 1 hour after each turn.

CUT INTO CROISSANTS

Roll out the dough into a rectangle 5mm thick. Use a large knife to cut the dough into equilateral triangles with 20cm sides and a 10cm base. Gently stretch the point of each dough triangle up from the base then roll up from the base to the top using the palms of both hands, delicately stretching the dough out to the side points without pressing or crushing or sticking the layers together. The top of the triangle should now be at the bottom of the croissant.

ALLOW THE CROISSANTS TO 'GROW'

Lay each croissant on a baking tray lined with a sheet of baking parchment then allow to grow at room temperature for about two and a half hours, covering them with a second sheet of baking parchment to stop them drying out. To keep them sufficiently moist, you can also brush the surface of the croissants with a little warm water. At the end of the rising time, the croissants should have added an extra 80% to their volume, but no more.

TO BAKE

Preheat the oven to 210°C (gas mark 6 to 7). Brush the croissants with beaten egg to glaze. Put the croissants in the oven for 10 to 12 minutes, according to the power of your oven, placing a bowl of cold water on the baking tray. Make sure you don't open the oven while they are cooking. When they are done, put them on a wire rack to cool.

Tangy Windmills

For about 15 windmills
Preparation time: 45mins
Resting time: 4hours
Refrigeration time: 5hours
Cooking time: 20 to 25mins

FOR THE LEAVEN
4 tablespoons water
40g fresh yeast
150g flour

FOR THE DOUGH
340g type 45 flour
8g table salt
55g caster sugar
85g butter, melted
15g fresh yeast
85ml water

250g butter
1 whole egg, to glaze

FOR THE LEAVEN
Knead the flour, water and yeast and allow to ferment at room temperature for 1 hour.

KNEAD THE DOUGH
Pour the leaven into the bowl of an electric mixer then cover with the flour, salt, sugar and the melted butter which should be cold when you add it to the dough.
Use the dough hook to combine everything on low speed for 2 minutes then immediately add the yeast, first dissolved in cold water.
Continue kneading on medium speed for another 6 minutes until the dough is homogenous.

ALLOW THE DOUGH TO REST
Leave the dough in the bowl and cover it with cling film so that the bowl is now fully airtight. This will stop the dough forming a crust.
Then leave the dough to rise at room temperature for 30 minutes.

PUT THE DOUGH IN THE FRIDGE
Bring the dough back to its initial ball-shape by kneading it gently by hand.
Put the ball on a sheet of baking parchment, cover with cling film and refrigerate for 2 hours.

ROLL OUT THE CREAMED BUTTER
Pound the butter between two sheets of baking parchment with a rolling pin then roll it out evenly into a 1cm thick rectangle.

GIVE THE PUFF PASTRY THREE TURNS
Roll out the dough to make a kind of cross. Place the rectangle of butter, which should be slightly smaller, in the middle and roll everything out to obtain a strip the width of which is a third of the length. Fold in the ends of the dough to make three overlapping layers like a folding wallet. Give the dough a quarter turn, wrap it in cling film, put it in the fridge for an hour and then give it a second turn exactly like the first.

Wrap the dough in cling film then allow to rest in the fridge for another hour. Finally, give it a third turn and put the dough in the fridge for one last hour.

TO FORM THE WINDMILLS
Roll out the dough to ½cm thick and use a large (quite long) knife to cut it into squares with 15 x 15cm sides then make cuts from each corner almost to the centre (up to two thirds but you need to leave the centre uncut).
Fold each corner to the left to form the 'sails' of the windmill.

ALLOW THE WINDMILLS TO GROW
Place the windmills on a sheet of baking parchment and allow to grow at room temperature for 2 hours 30 minutes (at 22 °C), placing a cup of warm water beside them and covering them with another sheet of baking parchment to stop them drying out and forming a crust.
When they have risen, the windmills should be 80% bigger, but no more.

FILL AND BAKE THE WINDMILLS
As you like, place preserved lemon, jam, crème pâtissière or compote in the centres.
Brush the dough with beaten egg to glaze.
Bake the windmills at 170°C (gas mark 3 to 4) for 20 to 25 minutes, according to your oven.
When they are done, lay them on a wire rack to cool.

Vanilla and Bergamot Follies

For about 15 follies
Preparation time: 50mins
Resting time: 2hours 30mins to
3hours
Cooking time: 30 to 35mins

FOR THE STREUSEL

50g slightly salted butter

50g type 45 flour

50g brown sugar (cassonade, see
   page 201)

65g ground hazelnuts

2 pinches fleur de sel

FOR THE DOUGH

200ml water

2 level tablespoons milk powder
   (12g)

25g yeast

400g type 55 flour

40g brown sugar (cassonade)

1 level tablespoon fleur de sel

40g thick cream

50g unsalted butter

2 scraped vanilla pods

FOR THE FILLING

brown sugar (cassonade)

100g crème pâtissière (see page
   211)

candied bergamot peel (available
   from delicatessens)

Zest of 1 orange

1 egg, to glaze

FOR THE STREUSEL

Take the butter out of the fridge 30 minutes beforehand. In a mixing bowl, combine the dry ingredients (flour, brown sugar, salt and ground hazelnuts) then add the slightly salted butter cut into chunks. Knead everything with your hands until the butter adheres to the dry ingredients without forming a dough. You should obtain a crumble-like mixture.

START KNEADING THE DOUGH

Combine the water and the milk powder. Warm the milk solution then pour it into the bowl of an electric mixer with the yeast.

Add the flour, brown sugar, salt and thick cream. Start to knead using the dough hook and complete this process in three separate stages. The first 5 minutes are to form the dough and make it stretchy. For that, you should start off gently on the first speed. After 5 minutes, switch to medium speed to 'create the gluten network' or the bread's internal structure, in other words, so that the gluten fibres in the flour agglomerate. This process is essential to obtain light, airy dough and will take another 5 minutes.

THIRD KNEADING STAGE

The third and last kneading stage is to make these pastries soft and moist by adding the butter. Start by melting the butter in a bain-marie. Then incorporate it a third at a time while still warm, switching the mixer back to low speed for the purpose. When the dough starts to come away from the sides of the bowl, quickly incorporate the vanilla seeds.

ALLOW THE BALLS OF DOUGH TO REST

Place the dough on the work surface then cut it into chunks weighing 70g each and roll the chunks into balls between lightly floured hands. Lay the balls of dough on a tray lined with baking parchment and allow to rest at room temperature for two and a half to three hours for the yeast to act. Place a piece of cling film over them.

FILL AND BAKE THE FOLLIES

Finely slice the bergamot zests then mix the crème pâtissière with the bergamot and orange zest. When the balls of dough have puffed up, brush them all over with beaten egg. Insert the nozzle (plain, n°8) of a piping bag into the middle of each ball and fill them with a generous knob of bergamot crème pâtissière. Scatter streusel over the centre of the follies and put them in the oven at 170°C (gas mark 3 to 4) for 30 to 35 minutes.

Vanilla and Sultana Briochins

For 15 people
Preparation time: 1hour 20mins
Resting time: 22hours
Cooking time: 30mins

100g brioche dough (see page 30)

200g vanilla crème pâtissière (see page 211)

Flour, for the work surface

FOR THE SULTANAS IN SYRUP

200ml water

40ml rum

50g caster sugar

30g sultanas

FOR THE BRIOCHE DOUGH AND SULTANAS IN SYRUP

The day before: make the brioche dough (see page 30), wrap it in cling film and put it in the fridge. In a small saucepan over a medium heat, heat the water, rum and sugar. Take the pan off the heat when the mixture boils and pour the syrup over the sultanas in a Pyrex® mixing bowl. Cover with cling film and allow to marinate in the fridge over night.

ROLL OUT THE DOUGH

The day before: prepare the crème pâtissière (see page 211). On a floured work surface, roll out the brioche dough into a square 5mm thick. Wrap it in cling film and put it in the fridge for 30 minutes for it to firm up slightly.

FILL THE DOUGH AND ROLL IT UP

Take the dough out of the fridge and brush the edges with the vine-fruit syrup. Now spread the crème pâtissière to within 1cm of the edges and scatter the drained sultanas over the cream. Starting from the top edge, roll up the dough tightly without leaving any space between the dough and the fruit. Use the syrup to stick the bottom edge of the dough to the rest of the dough then put the roll in the fridge for 20 minutes, taking care that the 'seal' holds underneath.

CUT THE BRIOCHINS

Cut the sausage of dough into 15 pieces 4cm long then arrange them in staggered rows (leaving enough space between them) on a baking tray lined with baking parchment. Press them down delicately with the palm of your hand and cover with cling film then allow to rest at room temperature for two hours until the briochins puff up as the yeast ferments.

TO BAKE

Preheat the oven to 170°C (gas mark 3 to 4). Bake the brioches in the oven for about 15 minutes. Allow to cool on a wire rack before serving.

Apple and Honey Spread

For about 600g
Preparation time: 20mins
Cooking time: 30mins

500g Golden Delicious apples

50g butter

100g runny honey (any kind of flower)

Juice of 1 small lemon

100g apple juice (green, if possible)

1 level teaspoon ground cinnamon

2 generous pinches fleur de sel

FOR THE FRUIT
Peel, core then finely dice the apples.

COOK THE 'CARAMEL'
In a frying pan, melt the butter over a medium heat until foaming then add the honey. Whisk in the lemon juice and apple juice. Bring to the boil and cook for 1 minute.

FOR THE CANDIED APPLE CUBES
Now add the diced apple to the pan and cook for about 7 to 8 minutes over a low heat. Sprinkle with cinnamon and fleur de sel then continue cooking over a low heat for 15 to 20 minutes, stirring from time to time to prevent the mixture sticking. The apples should not caramelise at this stage but they should reduce.

FOR THE CARAMEL
Turn up the heat and continue cooking until caramelisation occurs. Allow the diced apple to cool at room temperature.

BLEND THE CREAM
Put the candied apples in the bowl of an electric mixer then blend to obtain a smooth, thick paste. Store in the fridge and serve cold like jam as an accompaniment to viennoiseries.

TEATIME TREATS

Marbled Chocolate and Hazelnut Cake

For 6 to 7 people
Preparation time: 25mins
Cooking time: 35mins

2 egg whites

90g brown sugar (cassonade, see
   page 201)

90g ground hazelnuts

30g icing sugar

2 pinches fleur de sel

1 whole egg

½ egg yolk

85g butter (+ a little for the tin)

45g type 45 flour (+ a little for
the tin)

1 level teaspoon baking powder

15g cocoa powder

70g dark chocolate squares

20g pearl sugar (sugar nibs)

WHISK THE EGG WHITES

Gently whisk the egg whites to soft peaks, incorporating 30g of the brown sugar at the start. The mixture should be frothy but not too stiff.

COMBINE THE INGREGIENTS FOR THE DOUGH

In a mixing bowl, combine the ground hazelnuts, the rest of the brown sugar, the icing sugar and the fleur de sel. Add the whole egg and the egg yolk. Whisk vigorously for 30 seconds.

In a saucepan, melt the butter over a medium heat then cook for 1 to 2 minutes whisking constantly until it develops a nutty colour and flavour. At the end of the cooking time, the butter's lactic ferments should be a nice brown colour. Pour the butter into the previous mixture then stir in the sifted flour and baking powder half at a time.

Finally, incorporate the whisked egg whites half at a time. The dough should be airy and pliable.

TO FLAVOUR THE DOUGH

Take a quarter of the dough you have made and put it in a bowl. Stir in the cocoa powder with a spatula then fill a piping bag with a large plain nozzle with the mixture. Coarsely crush the dark chocolate squares and stir them delicately into the remaining dough, still with the spatula.

FILL THE LOAF TIN

Preheat the oven to 170°C (gas mark 3 to 4). Butter and flour a loaf tin, a loose-base cake tin or, better still, a 16 to 18cm cake ring placed on a baking tray lined with baking parchment. Sprinkle the base with sugar nibs and pour in the dough containing the dark chocolate squares to within 1cm from the top of the tin. Using the piping bag, pipe a generous spiral of the chocolate dough on top.

TO BAKE

Bake for about 30 minutes. The time will depend on your oven. To check whether the cake is done, insert the point of a knife, which should come out clean. Don't bake the cake for too long, however, because it should remain moist. Take the cake out of the oven and allow to cool for 5 minutes before turning it out.

Vanilla Flan

For 4 to 5 people
Preparation time: 25mins
Infusion time: 1hour
Refrigeration time: 30mins
Freezing: 2hours
Cooking time: 1hour

200g puff pastry (see page 209)
   (or rich short crust pastry–pâte
   brisée)
450ml semi-skimmed milk
130ml single cream
4 vanilla pods
140g caster sugar
45g cornflour
4 egg yolks
2 whole eggs
Flour and butter for the tin

BOIL THE MILK AND CREAM
In a saucepan covered with cling film, gently bring the milk and single cream to the boil with the split and scraped vanilla pods. Take off the heat then allow to infuse for 1 hour.

COMBINE THE REST OF THE INGREDIENTS
In a mixing bowl, combine the caster sugar and cornflour with the egg yolks and whole eggs then whisk vigorously until pale.
Bring the vanilla infusion back to the boil, this time without the cling film, then pour it in one go into the bowl containing the sweetened egg yolks. Whisk everything for the mixture to thicken. The cream should generously coat a wooden spoon. Cover the bowl with cling film, then allow to cool in the fridge until needed.

ROLL OUT THE PASTRY
Roll out the pastry to 5mm thick then use it to line a round, buttered and floured 16cm tin with sides 3 to 4cm high. Put the tin in the fridge for 30 minutes for the pastry to harden.

POUR THE MIXTURE INTO THE PASTRY CASE
Take the tin out of the fridge and pour in the mixture to within 3mm of the rim. Put the custard to set in the freezer for 2 hours.

TO BAKE
Preheat the oven to 170°C (gas mark 3 to 4). Bake the custard for 40 to 45 minutes. The cooking time depends on your oven. You can check whether the custard is done by inserting the point of a knife, which should come out clean. Allow to cool at room temperature and serve the custard while just warm for maximum creaminess on the palate! But it is just as good served cold.

Chocolate Sponge Cake

For 6 to 7 people
Preparation time: 25mins
Cooking time: 30mins

110g dark chocolate
20g milk cooking chocolate
70g butter (+ a little for the tin)
3 egg whites
90g brown sugar
90g ground hazelnuts
20g icing sugar
1 generous pinch fleur de sel
1 egg
1 egg yolk
40g type 45 flour (+ a little for the tin)
½ teaspoon baking powder
20g pearl sugar (sugar nibs)

MELT THE CHOCOLATE
Break up the milk chocolate and 40g of the dark chocolate, cut the butter into chunks, then melt everything in a bain-marie.

WHISK THE EGG WHITES
Gently whisk the egg whites to soft peaks, incorporating 15g of brown sugar at the start, until frothy but not too stiff.

COMBINE THE DRY INGREDIENTS
In a mixing bowl, combine the ground hazelnuts, the rest of the brown sugar, the icing sugar and the fleur de sel. Add the whole egg and the egg yolk. Whisk vigorously for about 30 seconds then add the melted chocolate half at a time and the sifted flour and baking powder. Incorporate the whisked egg whites half at a time, and as you do, add the rest of the chopped dark chocolate. The cake dough should be airy and pliable.

FILL THE TIN
Preheat the oven to 160°C (gas mark 3). Butter and flour a loaf tin, a loose-base cake tin or, better still, a 16 to 18cm cake ring placed on a baking tray lined with baking parchment. Scatter sugar nibs over the base and pour in the dough.

TO BAKE
Bake for about 20 to 25 minutes. The time depends on your oven. To check whether the cake is done, insert the point of a knife, which should come out clean. Don't bake the cake for too long, however, because it should stay moist. Take the cake out of the oven and allow to cool in the tin for 5 minutes before turning it out.

Dreamy Madeleines

For about 20 madeleines
Preparation time: 20mins
Resting time: 4hours
Cooking time: 25mins

135g butter (+ a bit for the
  moulds)
1 vanilla pod
3 eggs (150g)
140g caster sugar
2 pinches fleur de sel
2 teaspoons runny honey (any
  flower)
1 tablespoon peanut oil
125g flour
2 teaspoons (11g) baking powder
50ml semi-skimmed milk at room
  temperature

HEAT THE BAKING TRAY
Preheat the oven to 160°C (gas mark 3) with the tray inside. Caution: the baking sheet must be very hot when you place the madeleine tray on it (for the humps to form).

COMBINE THE INGREDIENTS
Melt the butter in a small saucepan and allow to warm slightly. If you have a thermometer, use it to measure 40°C. Split the vanilla pod in two and scrape out the seeds. In a mixing bowl, whisk together the whole eggs, the caster sugar, fleur de sel, honey and the vanilla pod seeds until the mixture is pale.
Now, add the peanut oil, the sifted flour and baking powder then the melted butter. When everything is thoroughly combined, pour in the milk.

ALLOW THE BATTER TO REST
Cover the madeleine batter with cling film then allow to rest in the fridge for at least 3 or 4 hours.

BAKE THE MADELEINES
Butter a flexible madeleine tray and use a piping bag (or a tablespoon) to fill the shells two-thirds full with the batter, then bake (on the hot baking sheet) for about 20 minutes. Allow the madeleines to cool slightly before turning them out of the shells.

Coconut, Ginger and Crunchy Sugar Cake

For 6 to 7 people
Preparation time: 25mins
Cooking time: 35mins

2 egg whites

90g brown sugar

90g ground coconut (coconut
   flour)

30g icing sugar

45g crystallised ginger

2 pinches fleur de sel

1 whole egg

½ egg yolk

85g butter (+ a bit for the tin)

45g type 45 flour (+ a bit for the
   tin)

1 level teaspoon baking powder

20g pearl sugar (sugar nibs)

1 heaped tablespoon grated
   coconut

WHISK THE EGG WHITES
Gently whisk the egg whites to soft peaks, incorporating 30g of the brown sugar at the start, until frothy but not too stiff.

COMBINE THE INGREDIENTS FOR THE DOUGH
In a mixing bowl, combine the ground coconut, the remaining brown sugar, the icing sugar, the finely diced ginger and the fleur de sel. Add the whole egg and the yolk. Whisk vigorously for about 30 seconds.
In a saucepan, melt the butter over a medium heat and cook for 1 to 2 minutes, whisking constantly until it develops a nutty colour and flavour. At the end of the cooking time, the butter's lactic ferments should be nice brown colour. Pour it into the previous mixture then incorporate the sifted flour and baking powder, half at a time.

FILL THE LOAF TIN
Preheat the oven to 170°C (gas mark 3 to 4). Butter and flour a loaf tin, a loose-base cake tin or, better still, a 16 to 18cm cake ring placed on a baking tray lined with baking parchment. Scatter sugar nibs and grated coconut over the base, then pour in the dough to within 1cm of the top of the tin.

TO BAKE
Bake for about 30 minutes. The time will depend on your oven. To check whether the cake is done, insert the point of a knife, which should come out clean. Don't bake the cake for too long, however, because it should remain moist. Take the cake out of the oven and allow to cool for 5 minutes before turning it out.

Conversation... Lemon and Hazelnut

For 8 people
Preparation time: 40mins
Refrigeration time: 2hours
Cooking time: 1hour 20mins

350g or flan pastry – pâte à fon-
  cer (see page 214)
Butter for the moulds

FOR THE CANDIED LEMON
4 organic lemons
250ml lemon juice
150g caster sugar

FOR THE HAZELNUT CREAM
90g butter
70g brown sugar
100g ground hazelnuts
2 eggs
20ml single cream
2 pinches fleur de sel

FOR THE SUGAR AND LEMON
  ICING
150g icing sugar
1 egg white
Zest of 1 lemon
1 drizzle lemon juice
1 pinch fleur de sel

FOR THE TARTLET SHELLS
Lightly butter 8cm tartlet rings or tins. Roll out
the pastry to ½cm thick and cut out 8 rounds
about 12cm in diameter then lay each pastry
round in the rings or tins pressing them into the
edges with your thumbs.
Cut out 8 more 8cm pastry rounds and strips
about 10cm long and ½cm wide. Put everything in
the fridge for at least 2 hours.

BLANCH THE LEMON ZESTS
Wash the lemons then, using a paring knife,
remove the peel leaving as little pith as you can
because the pith is extremely bitter. Immerse the
lemon rind in a pan half-full of water and bring to
the boil to blanch. Empty the pan through a sieve
and repeat the process twice more. The bitterness
is concentrated in the rind. By blanching the zest
three times, you are making sure the candied
lemon will not be too bitter.

FOR THE CANDIED LEMON
In a saucepan, cook the lemon rinds with the
lemon juice and sugar over a medium heat
(simmering), for 40 to 50 minutes. When the liquid
is sufficiently reduced (you should be left with
no more than a few tablespoons of juice), blend
everything in an electric mixer. Caution: this
mixture has an intense and concentrated citrus
flavour.

FOR THE HAZELNUT CREAM
Whisk the softened butter and brown sugar in
a mixing bowl. Add the ground hazelnuts then
the eggs one at a time. Finally, incorporate the
single cream and the fleur de sel. Whisk vigorously
for about 30 seconds to emulsify and produce a
smooth cream. Set aside.

FOR THE LEMON AND SUGAR ICING
Put the icing sugar in a bowl. Vigorously whisk in
the egg white and lemon zest then incorporate the
lemon juice and fleur de sel. Set aside.

TO ASSEMBLE THE TARTLETS AND BAKE
Two-thirds fill the tartlet shells with the hazelnut
cream, place a teaspoon of the candied lemon on
top then cover each tartlet with an 8cm round of
pastry and seal it like a pie.
Use a palette knife to spread the lemon and sugar
icing over the tartlets then arrange the pastry strips
in a lattice pattern on top to finish.
Bake at 170°C (gas mark 3 to 4) for half an hour,
according to your oven, until pastry and icing turn
golden brown.

Bittersweet Orange Cake

For 6 to 7 people
Preparation time: 35mins
Cooking time: 1hour 45mins

2 egg whites
90g brown sugar (cassonade, see page 201)
90g ground almonds
30g icing sugar
Grated zest of 2 organic oranges
1 vanilla pod
2 pinches fleur de sel
1 whole egg
½ egg yolk
85g butter (+ a bit for the tin)
45g type 45 flour (+ a bit for the tin)
1 level teaspoon baking powder
20g pearl sugar (sugar nibs)

FOR THE CANDIED ORANGE
3 or 4 organic oranges
75g sugar

FOR THE CANDIED ORANGE

Wash the oranges and remove the peel leaving as little white pith as you can. Squeeze them and reserve the juice. Weigh out 50g orange peel and measure out 125ml of the juice.
Put the orange peel into a saucepan, cover with cold water and bring to the boil. Empty the pan through a sieve and reserve the peel. Return them to the pan and repeat the process twice more.

FOR THE CANDIED PEEL

Put the blanched peel back in the pan and add the orange juice and the sugar. Cook over a low heat for about 40 to 50 minutes.
Blend the mixture.
This mixture has an intense and concentrated flavour.

WHISK THE EGG WHITES

Gently whisk the egg whites to soft peaks, incorporating 30g of the brown sugar at the start, until frothy but not too stiff.

COMBINE THE INGREDIENTS FOR THE DOUGH

In a mixing bowl, combine the ground almonds, the remaining brown sugar, the icing sugar, three quarters of the candied orange, the orange zest, the split vanilla pod with the seeds scraped out and the fleur de sel. Add the whole egg and the yolk. Whisk vigorously for about 30 seconds.
In a saucepan, melt the butter over a medium heat and cook for 1 to 2 minutes, whisking constantly until it develops a nutty colour and flavour. At the end of the cooking time, the butter's lactic ferments should be a nice brown colour. Pour it into the previous mixture then incorporate the sifted flour and baking powder half at a time.
Finally, incorporate the frothy egg whites half at a time. Start by whisking in a third to soften the dough, then stir in the other two thirds delicately and carefully with a spatula until fluffy and pliable with a ribbon consistency.

FILL THE LOAF TIN

Preheat the oven to 170°C (gas mark 3 to 4). Butter and flour a loaf tin, a loose-base cake tin or, better still, a 16 to 18cm cake ring placed on a baking tray lined with baking parchment. Scatter sugar nibs over the base and pour in half the dough. Now add the remaining candied orange and pour in the remaining cake dough to within 1cm of the top.

TO BAKE

Bake for about 30 minutes. The time will depend on your oven. To check whether the cake is done, insert the point of a knife, which should come out clean. Don't bake the cake for too long, however, because it should remain moist. Take the cake out of the oven and allow to cool in the tin for 5 minutes before turning it out.

Gâteaux Bretons with Brown Sugar

For 7 to 8 cakes
Preparation time: 30mins
Cooking time: 20mins

240g slightly salted butter (+ a bit
for the tin)
240g caster sugar
3 egg yolks
1 pinch fleur de sel
300g flour
1 pinch baking powder
1 tablespoon rum

TO DECORATE
1 egg yolk
Coffee extract

COMBINE THE INGREDIENTS
In a large mixing bowl, soften the butter by kneading it with a wooden spoon. When it is creamed, add the sugar and stir to a smooth consistency. Now incorporate the 3 egg yolks one at a time and the fleur de sel then gradually sift in the flour and baking powder together. Knead the dough, gradually adding the rum, until homogenous.

FOR THE TINS
Butter small cake rings 8 to 9cm in diameter and arrange them on your oven baking tray lined with baking parchment. Otherwise, you can use tartlet trays with shells of the same diameter. By hand, divide up the dough between the moulds to 1cm high, then smooth over the tops with your thumb or the back of a tablespoon dipped in hot water.

TO GLAZE
Preheat the oven to 170°C (gas mark 3 to 4). Beat the last egg yolk in a bowl with a drop of coffee extract, then brush the top of the cakes with the beaten egg.

TO BAKE
Bake for about 20 minutes. The baking time will depend on your oven. Check the cakes are a fine golden colour but still pliable. Wait 4 to 5 minutes then turn them out of the moulds before cold.

SALON DE THÉ

Creamed Rice

For 6 people
Preparation time: 15mins
Refrigeration time: 12hours
Cooking time: 25mins

80g pudding rice
750ml semi-skimmed milk
350ml single cream
45g caster sugar
3 vanilla pods

FOR THE VANILLA INFUSION

The day before: bring a pan of milk to the boil with the single cream, the sugar and the split and scraped vanilla pods.

Take the pan off the heat and allow to cool, then allow to infuse in the fridge till next day to draw out the flavours.

BLANCH THE RICE

The same day: tip the pudding rice into a saucepan and add enough cold water to cover. Bring to the boil, stirring with a wooden spoon. Immediately, take it off the heat then strain the rice through a sieve. Cool it instantly by putting it under the cold tap. The rice will not yet be cooked, just blanched: the outer layer covering the grains of rice will have split from the heat and the rice will thus have lost much of its starch and floury flavour.

TO COOK

Cook the rice in the vanilla-infused milk over a low heat. Make sure you leave the vanilla pods in for 15 to 20 minutes until the rice is tender. Caution: the rice should stay quite runny because it will go on absorbing the milk. Creamed rice can be served chilled or slightly warm… as you like it.

Floating Islands, Vanilla and Praline

For 6 people
Preparation time: 40mins
Cooking time: 20mins
Refrigeration time: 3 or 4hours

FOR THE CRÈME ANGLAISE
375ml semi-skimmed milk
6 egg yolks
120g caster sugar
2 vanilla pods

FOR THE FLOATING ISLANDS
160g brown sugar
(or white sugar)
2 vanilla pods
4 egg whites
20g (approx) icing sugar

120g praline paste
(see page 172)

FOR THE CRÈME ANGLAISE
Make the crème anglaise in the morning for the evening, or the day before for the next day.
In a saucepan, bring the milk to the boil with the split and scraped vanilla pods. Meanwhile, whisk the egg yolks with the sugar until thick and pale (about 2 minutes).
When the milk boils, take it off the heat and pour it over the mixture of eggs and sugar a half or third at a time, continuing to whisk vigorously.

TO COOK THE CRÈME ANGLAISE
Return the mixture to the pan over a medium heat and stir with a wooden spatula in a figure of 8, stirring constantly to prevent the yolks from coagulating. The mixture will gradually thicken and the bubbles disappear. You will feel the cream forming under your spatula (don't be afraid to take the pan off the heat, continuing to stir, if it thickens up too fast). The key to a luscious creamy consistency is in the cooking. You need to bring the mixture to just below boiling point without at any stage letting it boil.
Remember: cook the mixture as much as possible without letting it boil.

PUT THE CRÈME ANGLAISE IN THE FRIDGE
When the crème anglaise is cooked, strain it, whisk for 30 seconds and allow to cool at room temperature, stirring from time to time.
When the mixture is cold, cover it with cling film and allow to thicken and mature in the fridge for 3 or 4 hours.

FOR THE MERINGUE ISLANDS
Whisk together the brown sugar, the seeds from the split and scraped vanilla pods and the egg whites to form stiff frothy peaks.

BAKE THE FLOATING ISLANDS
Use a pastry brush to butter moulds of whatever shape you choose (they should be the size of a tennis ball).
Using a piping bag or, failing that, a stainless steel spatula, fill the moulds with the whisked egg whites, taking care not to leave air pockets. Place them on your oven baking tray and bake at 140°C/150°C (gas mark 1 to 2) for 15 minutes. Allow the islands (which will soon be 'floating') to cool in the moulds then carefully turn them out on to a sheet of baking parchment.

ASSEMBLE THE FLOATING ISLANDS
To assemble, pour the chilled crème anglaise into a container of your choice, sprinkle icing sugar evenly over the meringue and sit the meringue on the crème anglaise. At the last minute, pour the praline over the chilled cream all around the floating island.

Crème Caramel

For 6 people
Preparation time: 30mins
Cooking time: 1hour
Refrigeration time: at least 6hours

FOR THE CARAMEL
250g caster sugar
2 tablespoons water

FOR THE EGG CUSTARD
150g caster sugar
5 small eggs or 4 large ones
   (200g)
3 egg yolks (60g)
2 vanilla pods
1litre semi-skimmed milk

FOR THE CARAMEL
In a saucepan over a medium heat, heat 150g of the sugar with the 2 tablespoons water. When the sugar turns a dark copper colour, take it off the heat and immediately stop the cooking process by standing the pan in cold water. Pour the caramel into 6 ramekins so that it covers the bottom. Sit the ramekins in a gratin dish with water surrounding them.

COMBINE THE CUSTARD INGREDIENTS
In a mixing bowl, combine the sugar, eggs, egg yolks and the split and scraped vanilla pods. Whisk until pale. Now pour in the cold milk and whisk again, then let the custard rest for 10 minutes until the surface bubbles have disappeared. Skim lightly with a tablespoon so that the custard is clear.

POUR THE CUSTARD INTO THE RAMEKINS
Preheat the oven to 140°C (gas mark 1). Pour the custard into the ramekins to within 5mm of the rim. Lay a sheet of baking foil over the ramekins, then cook them in a bain-marie for about 1 hour, according to your oven. The custard is baked when it is slightly wobbly, neither too runny nor too firm. Insert a knife to be sure; if the blade comes out clean and is hot, the custards are done.

ALLOW TO COOL BEFORE YOU TURN THEM OUT
Put the custards in the fridge for at least 6 hours (24 is better) before carefully turning them out of the moulds. To do that, insert the blade of a knife between the baked custard and the mould and run it around the edge. Gently turn them out upside down into bowls or a serving dish, and above all, serve chilled!

Brown Sugar Waffles

For 8 waffles
Preparation time: 35mins
Resting time: 3hours 50mins
Cooking time: 24mins

310g flour
60g brown sugar
1 generous pinch fleur de sel
125 ml semi-skimmed milk
25g fresh yeast
2 small eggs (60g)
200g butter
130g sugar nibs

FOR THE BATTER

In the bowl of an electric mixer, use the dough hook to combine the dry ingredients (flour, brown sugar and fleur de sel). Dissolve the fresh yeast in the semi-skimmed milk then add it to the bowl followed by the whole eggs and butter at room temperature.

Mix for 10 minutes on medium speed. The batter should be smooth, homogenous and elastic.

INCORPORATE THE SUGAR NIBS

Cover the batter (in the bowl) with a clean cloth and allow it to rise for 30 minutes. Then add the sugar nibs (still with the dough hook) so that they are evenly distributed throughout the batter. Set aside in the fridge for 2 hours.

ROLL OUT THE BATTER

Roll out the waffle batter between two sheets of baking parchment to 1cm thick. Allow to rest again in the fridge for 30 minutes.

CUT THE BATTER

When the batter is firm and quite hard, cut it into oval-shaped discs and allow to rise for another 40 minutes (it should nearly double in volume).

Cook the puffed-up batter discs in an aluminium waffle maker, checking that the waffles are golden and soft in the middle.

Chocolate Mousse

For 6 people
Preparation time: 20mins
Cooking time: 5mins
Refrigeration time: 3hours

300g dark chocolate
80g butter
2 egg yolks
7 egg whites
50g brown sugar

MELT THE CHOCOLATE
Break up the chocolate into chunks and dice the butter. Tip the pieces into a Pyrex® bowl and sit the bowl in a saucepan of water. Melt the butter and chocolate in a bain-marie over a low heat. Meanwhile, put the egg yolks in a bowl, and when the butter and chocolate have melted and are well combined, pour the mixture over the egg yolks half at a time. Whisk vigorously the whole time to form an emulsion.

WHISK THE EGG WHITES
Pour the brown sugar and egg whites into a large bowl or, better still, a small freestanding mixer. Whisk until frothy and the peaks hold their shape but above all are not too stiff.

COMBINE THE TWO MIXTURES
Using a wooden spoon or spatula, delicately stir the egg whites into the chocolate emulsion half at a time. Gently pour the mousse into the receptacle or receptacles of your choice then chill for at least 3 hours. The mousse gets its light, foamy consistency from the resting time in the fridge.

White Chocolate Lava Cakes with Lemon

For about 6 to 8 lava cakes
6 to 7cm in diameter and 5cm high
Preparation time: 40mins
Cooking time: 50mins to 1hour
*   15mins*
Resting time: 15mins

FOR THE CANDIED LEMON

2 organic lemons

125 ml lemon juice

75g caster sugar

FOR THE LAVA CAKES

200g white chocolate

50g butter

20ml semi-skimmed milk

60g unsweetened evaporated milk

140g eggs (lightly beat 2 eggs
    before weighing)

40g rice flour

60g type 55 flour

BLANCH THE ZESTS

Wash the lemons then use a paring knife to remove the peel and as much of the white pith as you can, because the pith is extremely bitter. Put the peel into a small saucepan half-full of water then bring to the boil to blanch. Empty the pan through a sieve then repeat the process twice more.

The bitterness is concentrated in the peel; by blanching the zests three times, you are making sure the candied lemon will not be too bitter.

FOR THE CANDIED LEMON

In a saucepan, cook the lemon peel with the lemon juice and sugar over a medium heat (simmering), for 40 to 50 minutes. When the liquid is sufficiently reduced, blend everything in an electric mixer. Caution: this mixture has an intense and concentrated citrus flavour.

FOR THE LAVA CAKES

Melt the white chocolate and butter in a bain-marie, then heat the milks gently in a small pan without letting them boil. Meanwhile, whisk together the eggs and the two types of flour in a mixing bowl.

Still whisking, pour the hot milk over the melted white chocolate and butter, then pour this mixture over the eggs, whisking vigorously but briefly. You should obtain a smooth, homogenous mixture.

TO BAKE

Place buttered and floured rings (approximately 6 cm wide and 7cm high) on baking parchment on the dripping pan from your oven.

Pour in the mixture to about 1cm deep, then place 1 teaspoon of candied lemon in the centre without touching the edges. Finish with the chocolate mixture to within 1cm of the top of the rings. Allow to rest for 10 minutes then put the cakes to bake in the middle of the oven for 10 to 15 minutes at 180°C (gas mark 4).

The cooking time will depend in large part on your oven. The cakes should not be cooked right through so the centre stays runny.

TURN OUT THE CAKES

Wait 5 minutes before removing the rings. Serve the lava cakes slightly warm or hot: to die for!

Citrus Salad with a Tangy Jus

For 6 people
Preparation time: 45mins
Cooking time: 15mins
Refrigeration time: 6hours

FOR THE CITRUS FRUIT SEGMENTS

2 pink pomelos

1 grapefruit

4 juicing oranges
(seedless or almost)

6 clementines

3 mandarins

4 blood oranges

150g kumquats

FOR THE JUICE

400ml orange juice

400ml pink pomelo juice

200ml blood orange juice

80ml lime juice

100-150g brown sugar (vergeoise
   blonde, see page 201, or white)
   according to your taste

1 level teaspoon pain d'épices
   spice (or cinnamon)

1 star anise

1 vanilla pod

1 sprig lemon balm

5 sprigs fresh coriander

2 generous pinches fleur de sel

TO THICKEN

2 tablespoons cornflour

3 tablespoons cold water

FOR THE CITRUS FRUIT SEGMENTS

Peel all the citrus fruit and put it in a large mixing bowl. Leave in the mandarin seeds, halve the kumquats and remove the seeds. Separate the segments taking care to remove all the white pith, which would make this dessert bitter. Don't slice the segments away from the membranes, because you want the fruit to remain intact in the hot marinade and the membranes will give them a more syrupy texture.

REDUCE THE JUICES

Pour the fruit juices and two thirds of the brown sugar into a pan together with the star anise, the split and scraped vanilla pod, the sprig of lemon balm and the spices. Bring to the boil and start to reduce to concentrate the flavours.

Reduce the juice by at least a third over a medium heat but without boiling. Add the coriander and fleur de sel and season again with brown sugar if you wish. Reduce for another few minutes until you are only left with half the juice you started with.

THICKEN THE JUICE

Dilute the cornflour in the water. Gradually pour this mixture into the reduced juice while still simmering, whisking vigorously to thicken. Caution: you most certainly won't need all the water-cornflour mixture, but you should obtain a liquid, syrupy juice.

MARINATE THE CITRUS FRUIT

Take the pan off the heat and strain all the juice through a muslin cloth or fine-mesh sieve. Allow to cool for no more than 5 minutes, then pour it while still hot over the citrus fruit segments. Allow everything to marinate in the fridge for at least 6 hours and serve the citrus fruit salad chilled in soup bowls or another dish of your choice, without drowning the fruit in too much juice. Sprinkle with a hint of spice (pain d'épices or cinnamon).

Semolina Cake

For 7 to 8 people
Preparation time: 30mins
Cooking time: 45mins
Refrigeration time: 18hours

100g currants
120ml dark rum
150g durum wheat fine semolina
2 large eggs
2 pinches fleur de sel

FOR THE VANILLA INFUSION
800ml semi-skimmed milk
200ml single cream
110g white or brown sugar
3 vanilla pods

FOR THE CARAMEL
150g sugar
2 tablespoons water

FOR THE VANILLA INFUSION
The day before, boil the milk, cream, sugar and the split and scraped vanilla pods in a container of your choice. Allow to cool, cover with cling film and refrigerate overnight for the mixture to infuse in the vanilla and develop plenty of aromas.

MARINATE THE CURRANTS
Also the day before, put the currants to marinate in the rum, cover with cling film and refrigerate for the currants to swell up and absorb the rum flavour (the alcohol will evaporate during the cooking time).

FOR THE CARAMEL
The same day, pour 150g sugar and 2 tablespoons water into a saucepan over a medium heat. When the sugar turns a dark copper colour, immediately stop the cooking process by standing the pan in cold water. Pour the caramel into 6 ramekins so that it covers the bottom.

COOK THE SEMOLINA
Pour the vanilla infusion (leave the pods in) into a saucepan over a medium heat and bring to the boil. As soon as it starts to bubble, sprinkle the semolina in, stirring constantly with a wooden spoon or a spatula, then add the marinated currants with the rum and fleur de sel. Now, reduce the heat and simmer for about 6 to 7 minutes. When the mixture thickens but is still soft and creamy, take it off the heat.

INCORPORATE THE EGGS
Now add the eggs, stirring briskly to incorporate them thoroughly into the semolina cream, which should be smooth and homogenous.

FINISH COOKING IN A BAIN-MARIE
Preheat the oven to 140°C (gas mark 1). Fill a roasting tin with cold water, and, while the cream is still piping hot, pour it into the ramekins – or the mould of your choice – then sit the ramekins on a wire rack in a roasting tin full of water. Lay a sheet of baking foil over the ramekins, then bake in the oven in this bain-marie for 20 minutes.

REFRIGERATE FOR SEVERAL HOURS
Leave the semolina cakes in the fridge for at least 6 hours (24 is even better), before carefully turning them out of the mould by inserting the blade of a knife between the baked semolina and the mould and running it around the edge. Gently turn them out upside down on to the plates or serving dish, and above all, serve chilled!

Fruit Tagine

For 6 people
Preparation time: 25mins
Cooking time: 35mins

FOR THE FOAMING, TANGY BUTTER
30g butter
50g brown sugar (cassonade, see page 201)
1 vanilla pod (from Tahiti)
35ml lemon juice

FOR THE FRUIT
2 Golden Delicious apples
175g orange segments
175g pink pomelo segments
65g sultanas
25g whole blanched almonds
Juice of 1 grapefruit
Juice of 2 oranges
1 teaspoon vanilla extract
10g candied ginger, finely sliced
1 generous pinch ground cinnamon
1 pinch pain d'épices spice
40g brown sugar (cassonade)
10 fresh mint leaves

FOR THE FRUIT
Peel and core the apples then dice them finely. Segment the citrus fruit (orange and pomelos), removing all the white pith and taking care to catch the juice in a small bowl.

FOR THE FOAMING BUTTER
In a saucepan, melt the butter over a medium heat until foaming, then add the brown sugar and the split and scraped vanilla pod. Deglaze with the lemon juice, then stir the mixture carefully with a spatula until homogenous.

INCORPORATE THE FRUIT AND SPICES
Add the diced apples to the foaming butter then the sultanas and whole almonds. Reduce for 3 minutes over a medium heat, then add the orange and grapefruit segments. Continue cooking for another 2 minutes, then pour in half the grapefruit and orange juice, the vanilla extract, finely sliced candied ginger, the remaining sugar then the cinnamon and pain d'épices spice.

CONTINUE COOKING
Turn down the heat and reduce for about 20 minutes over a low heat, stirring occasionally to stop it sticking and moistening progressively with the remaining orange and grapefruit juice. At the end of the cooking time, take off the heat, and add the fresh mint leaves.

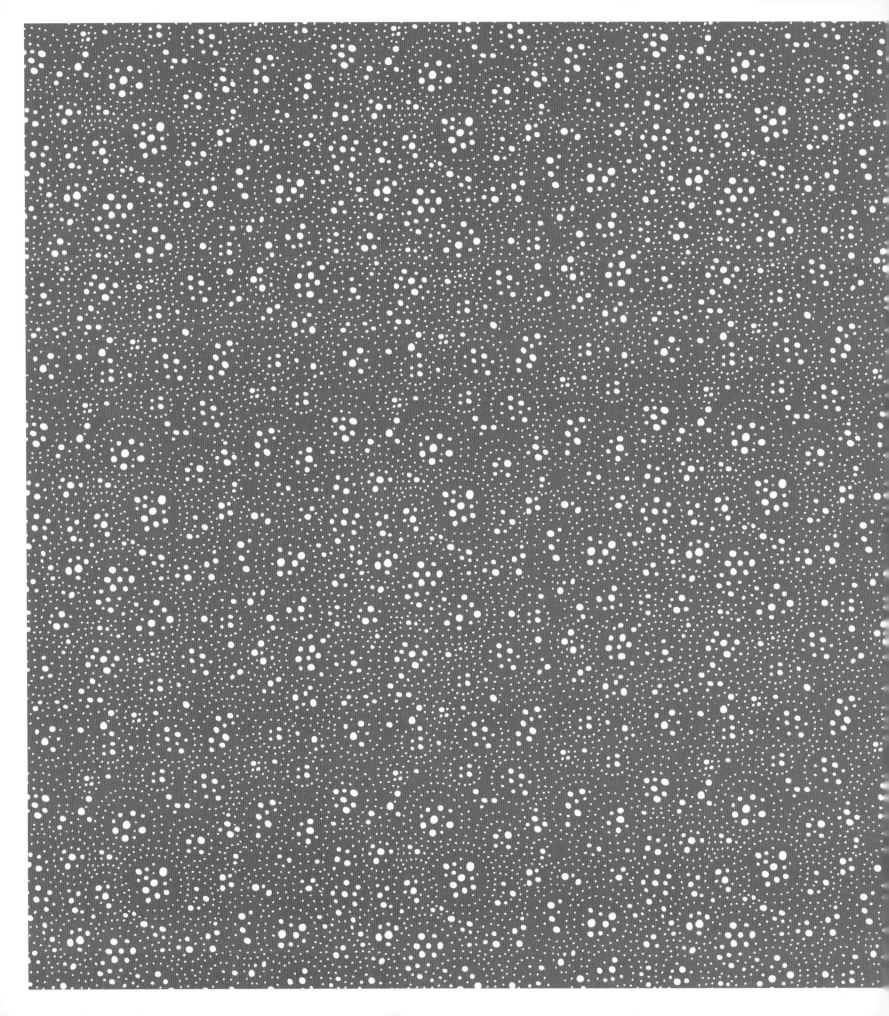

BISCUITS

Spicy Almond and Fruit Fondant Biscuits

For about 20 biscuits
Preparation time: 45mins
Refrigeration time: 12hours
Cooking time: 10mins

110ml rum
60g sultanas
170g butter
140g caster sugar
60g ground almonds
2 whole eggs (100g)
2 egg yolks (35g)
25ml semi-skimmed milk
75ml single cream
110g type 45 flour
90g fruit tajine (see page 213)

THE DAY BEFORE

Prepare the fruit tajine in a mixing bowl (see page 213). Put the rum and sultanas together in a bowl. Cover both bowls with cling film and refrigerate until next day.

FOR THE DOUGH

The same day, before starting this recipe, make sure all the ingredients are at room temperature. In a mixing bowl, cream the softened butter with a whisk. Add the sugar and ground almonds and whisk until pale.

Now incorporate the whole eggs and the yolks then stir again. Pour in the milk and single cream, then the marinated sultanas with the rum a little at a time. Finally, add the sifted flour half at a time. Beat the mixture briskly for about 15 seconds.

TO BAKE

Preheat the oven to 200°C (gas mark 6). Using a tablespoon, spoon the biscuit dough into silicone dariole moulds, 4 to 5cm in diameter and 4 to 5cm high, to three-quarters full. Place a spoonful of fruit tajine on each one.

Bake in the oven for 8 to 10 minutes then turn the biscuits out of the moulds while still warm.

Caramel and Crystallised Ginger Tuiles

For about 20 tuiles
Preparation time: 40mins
Refrigeration time: 1hour

FOR THE CARAMEL SAUCE
35ml single cream
25ml milk
3 tablespoons water
110g caster sugar
10g butter

FOR THE CARAMEL GANACHE
(minimum quantities for a smooth
    ganache)
65ml single cream
1 knob butter
3 tablespoons water
80g caster sugar
4g glucose
45g white chocolate
1 pinch fleur de sel

FOR THE TUILES BATTER
180g butter
4 whole eggs
4 egg whites
35g brown sugar (vergeoise
    blonde, see page 201)
90g type 55 flour
130g caramel sauce (recipe
    above)
30g caramel ganache (recipe
    above)

TO FINISH
A few grains fleur de sel
20g crystallised ginger

FOR THE CARMEL SAUCE
In a small saucepan, warm the cream and milk. Pour the water into another pan, add the caster sugar and cook over a medium heat. When the caramel turns a dark copper colour, gradually pour the hot cream and milk over it in a single stream, whisking constantly.
Continue cooking the caramel on a medium heat and bring to the boil for about 30 seconds. Finish by adding the butter off the heat.

FOR THE CARAMEL GANACHE
Warm the cream and butter in a small saucepan. Pour the water into another small pan, then add the caster sugar. Heat everything over a medium heat.
When the cooked sugar bubbles and reaches 125°C (use a kitchen thermometer), add the glucose. Continue cooking until the caramel turns a dark copper colour, then gradually pour the hot cream and butter over it in a single stream. Bring to the boil for about 30 seconds to make sure the mixture stays homogenous. Allow to cool off the heat then add the white chocolate, finely chopped beforehand, and the fleur de sel. Mix, then allow the caramel to cool at room temperature. The caramel will be thick but still pliable like a ganache. Pour it into a mixing bowl, cover with cling film then refrigerate until needed.

COMBINE THE INGREDIENTS FOR THE TUILES BATTER
Melt the butter in a small pan. In a mixing bowl, whisk together the whole eggs, egg whites and the sugar. Add the flour and melted butter, whisk vigorously, then incorporate 130g of the caramel

sauce and 30g caramel ganache. Whisk again, then allow the mixture to rest in the fridge for 1 hour.

ROLL OUT THE BATTER
Preheat the oven to 180°C (gas mark 4). Use the back of a tablespoon to spread a small amount of the tuiles batter as evenly and thinly as possible on a baking tray lined with baking parchment, forming ovals of the diameter of your choice. Sprinkle with a few grains of fleur de sel and tiny cubes of crystallised ginger.

TO BAKE
Put the tuiles in the oven until golden. Take them out of the oven and shape them over the rolling pin while still pliable to give them an attractive curve. Allow to cool before serving.

Praline Shortbread

For 6 or 7 people
Preparation time: 30mins
Refrigeration time: 1hour
Cooking time: 15mins

FOR THE SHORTBREAD

250g flour

125g butter

2 pinches fleur de sel

2 teaspoons (11g) baking powder

3 egg yolks

100g caster sugar

1 vanilla pod

FOR THE GIANDUJA

140g shelled hazelnuts

60g icing sugar

35g milk chocolate

2 squares dark chocolate

TO FINISH

30g shelled hazelnuts

FOR THE SHORTBREAD

Combine the flour, butter, salt and baking powder. Rub everything together with your fingertips to a crumbly consistency.

Whisk together the egg yolks and sugar with the seeds from the split and scraped vanilla pod. Add this emulsion to the butter and flour mixture and stir to obtain a homogenous dough.

Wrap in cling film and store in the fridge.

COOK THE BISCUITS

Roll out the dough to ½cm thick and use a round pastry cutter to cut out discs 6cm in diameter. Allow to rest for 1 hour in the fridge.

Bake in the oven at 170°C (gas mark 3 to 4) for about 12 to 15 minutes, according to your oven.

FOR THE GIANDUJA

In a food processor, pulse the hazelnuts with the icing sugar to a fine powder. Wait 10 minutes for the powder to cool (the mixture will be hot from the processing), then blend again to obtain a thick but runny paste.

In a bain-marie or in the microwave, melt the milk chocolate and dark chocolate, then pour the chocolate into the hazelnut paste and blend again to thoroughly incorporate everything and obtain the gianduja.

TO FINISH THE BISCUITS

Using a piping bag with a plain n° 8 nozzle, pipe regular mounds of gianduja in the middle of each biscuit leaving a 1cm border around the edge. The paste will slowly spread out. Scatter quite finely crushed hazelnuts over the top and put the biscuits in the fridge.

Bring them out 10 minutes before serving.

If you want, you can dip these biscuits in lukewarm dark chocolate to coat, as in the photo.

Soft Cantuccini

For about 20 biscuits
Preparation time: 30mins
Refrigeration time: 1hour
Cooking time: 25mins

125g marzipan

1 egg

1 egg yolk

35g ground almonds

15g very soft, slightly salted
   butter

2 tablespoons orange flower
   water

35g caster sugar

35g brown sugar (cassonade, see
   page 201)

Zest of 1 orange

20g preserved ginger

1 vanilla pod

1 level teaspoon pain d'épices
   spice (or cinnamon)

110g whole blanched almonds (or
   flaked almonds)

175g flour

1 level teaspoon baking powder

FOR THE DOUGH
In a mixing bowl, use a spatula to combine the marzipan with the whole egg and the egg yolk, then the ground almonds, very soft butter, the orange flower water and both sugars, the orange zest, the finely diced preserved ginger and the seeds from the split and scraped vanilla pod and the pain d'épices. Chop up the almonds coarsely with a knife or crush them with the rolling pin then stir them into the above mixture. Add the sifted flour and baking powder together. The dough you obtain should be pliable but firm.

ALLOW TO HARDEN IN THE FRIDGE
Put the dough between two sheets of baking parchment then use a rolling pin to knock it into a rectangle or a square 4 to 5cm thick. Put the dough in the fridge for 1 hour.

FOR THE FIRST COOK
Preheat the oven to 170°C (gas mark 3 to 4). Put the dough on a tray lined with baking parchment and bake for 15 minutes. Allow to cool to room temperature. Don't turn the oven off. Using a large knife, cut 1cm thick strips from the dough, then cut them again to make rectangles 10cm long by 3cm wide.

FOR THE SECOND BAKE
Lay the biscuits on a baking tray lined with baking parchment and bake again for 10 to 12 minutes.
Allow to cool before serving.

Langues de Chat with Green Tea and White Chocolate

For 6 to 7 people
Preparation time: 30mins
Cooking time: 10mins

FOR THE LANGUES DE CHAT

90g butter

90g caster sugar

1 generous pinch fleur de sel

1 small egg yolk

85g egg whites

15g white chocolate, melted

1 tablespoon thick cream, 40 % fat

7g Matcha green tea

90g type 55 flour

FOR THE FILLING

50g white chocolate

A few grains fleur de sel

FOR THE BISCUIT DOUGH

In a mixing bowl, whisk the softened butter with the sugar and fleur de sel, add the egg yolk, the egg whites, the melted white chocolate, thick cream and the green tea and finally the flour.

BAKE THE LANGUES DE CHAT

Line a baking tray with baking parchment. Spoon the mixture into a piping bag fitted with a 1cm round nozzle and pipe straight lines of the mixture, about 8cm long, onto the paper. Leave 5cm between each biscuit as they will spread during cooking. Bake at 150°C (gas mark 2) for 7 minutes. Loosen them when they come out of the oven and allow to cool.

ASSEMBLE THE BISCUITS

Gently melt two thirds of the white chocolate at not more than 45°C to 50°C then add the remaining chocolate. Whisk thoroughly to incorporate and reduce the temperature of the chocolate to about 26°C to 27°C (it should feel just warm on the lips). Spread a thin layer of the chocolate on a sheet of baking parchment and sprinkle with a few grains of fleur de sel. Cut the chocolate before it hardens into small, finger-size rectangles.

Sandwich together two green tea biscuits with the chocolate in between – extremely moreish!

Spicy Banana Tuiles with Black Sesame Seeds

For about 20 tuiles
Preparation time: 20mins
Refrigeration time: 1hour

160g butter
5 whole eggs
2 egg whites
220g icing sugar
95g brown sugar
70g type 55 flour
400g processed banana
1 teaspoon pain d'épices spice
10g black sesame seeds
A few grains fleur de sel

FOR THE TUILES

Melt the butter but don't let it get too hot.
In a mixing bowl, whisk together the whole eggs, the egg whites, the icing sugar and the brown sugar. Add the flour and melted butter, mix well, then use a spatula to incorporate the banana and pain d'épices spice. Allow to rest in the fridge for at least 1 hour.

FORM THE TUILES

Use the back of a tablespoon to spread a small amount of the tuiles batter evenly and thinly on a baking tray lined with baking parchment, forming ovals of the diameter you choose.
Sprinkle the tuiles with a few black sesame seeds and a few grains fleur de sel.

TO BAKE

Put the tuiles in the oven at 180°C (gas mark 4) and bake until golden.
Take them out of the oven and shape them over a rolling pin while still pliable to give them an attractive curve.

Tasty Shortbread

For about 20 biscuits
Preparation time: 55mins
Refrigeration time: 3hours 45mins
Cooking time: 35mins

FOR THE SHORTBREAD DOUGH

1 vanilla pod

150g very soft butter

85g brown sugar (cassonade, see page 201)

210g flour

30g wholewheat flour

2 teaspoons (11g) baking powder

1 level teaspoon fleur de sel

1 egg, beaten

TO COAT AND FILL

40g grated coconut

10g icing sugar

40g unsalted pistachios

40g ground almonds

40g ground hazelnuts

20g preserved ginger

100g dark chocolate

100g milk chocolate

Fleur de sel

COMBINE THE INGREDIENTS FOR THE DOUGH

Split the vanilla pod in two, scrape it out and reserve the seeds. In a mixing bowl, whisk the softened butter vigorously with the brown sugar to a smooth, homogenous mixture. Add the vanilla seeds, both types of flour, the fleur de sel and the baking powder. Mix thoroughly. Spread out the dough on a baking tray lined with baking parchment then refrigerate for 3 hours for the dough to harden.

CUT OUT THE BISCUITS

Roll out the dough again to 7 to 8mm thick. Using a pastry cutter or a glass to guide you, cut out rounds of dough 6cm in diameter then lay them on a baking tray lined with baking parchment.

GLAZE WITH BEATEN EGG

Use a pastry brush to brush the biscuits with beaten egg then put them in the fridge for 45 minutes.

Preheat the oven to 160°C (gas mark 3). Take the biscuits out of the fridge and brush with beaten egg a second time then bake in the oven for 15 minutes.

TOAST THE NUTS

Pulse the coconut to a fine powder then combine with 10g icing sugar. Now pulse to a fine powder the pistachios, ground almonds and ground hazelnuts. Spread out the powders on baking trays lined with baking parchment and put them in the oven for 10 to 12 minutes at 160°C (gas mark 3). Allow to cool to room temperature. Process the coconut powder with the preserved, finely diced ginger.

COAT THE BISCUITS

In separate bain-maries, melt the dark and milk chocolate. Use a small stainless steel palette knife to spread the dark chocolate over half the biscuits. While the chocolate is still soft, sprinkle a very few grains of fleur de sel on top, then lay some of the biscuits, chocolate-side down, in the pistachio powder and the others in the almond powder to give them a light coating of nuts. Tap them gently to remove the surplus.

Repeat this process to cover the remaining biscuits with milk chocolate, adding a few grains fleur de sel then placing half in the hazelnut powder and the other half in the coconut and ginger powder. Enjoy!

Coconut Snaps

For about 20 snaps
Preparation time: 10mins
Cooking time: 10mins

10g butter

1 tablespoon honey

3 level tablespoons brown sugar

60g grated coconut

1 egg white

FOR THE DOUGH

Melt the butter and honey then add the sugar and grated coconut. When the mixture has cooled to room temperature, stir in the egg white.

TO BAKE

Roll out the mixture as thinly as possible between two sheets of baking parchment. Cut into preferred shape and size.

Bake in the oven at 160°C (gas mark 3) for about 5 to 6 minutes until they turn a caramel colour.

Ladyfingers with Matcha Tea

For 6 or 7 people
Preparation time: 30mins
Resting time: 15mins
Cooking time: 10 to 12mins

65g egg yolks
95g caster sugar
65g type 55 flour
25g cornflour
2 pinches fleur de sel
1 tablespoon semi-skimmed milk
95g egg whites
8g Matcha green tea
Icing sugar

FOR THE BATTER

In a mixing bowl, whisk together the egg yolks with two thirds of the sugar until pale, light and fluffy with a ribbon consistency. Use a spatula to stir in the flour then the cornflour without overworking the mixture then add the fleur de sel and the milk.

WHISK THE EGG WHITES

Whisk up the egg whites, adding the remaining sugar half-way through to form stiff peaks. The meringue mixture should be firm, smooth and pliable.

Delicately fold the whisked egg whites into the previous mixture half at a time together with the green tea.

TO ASSEMBLE THE BISCUITS

Line a baking tray with baking parchment. Stick the paper down with a knob of the mixture you obtained at each corner.

You can also lightly butter and generously flour the baking tray then rap the tray to remove any excess flour.

Using a piping bag with a n° 10 plain nozzle, pipe biscuits (not too thick) about 10cm long in staggered rows for optimal cooking.

TO BAKE

Sprinkle the biscuits with icing sugar and allow this first layer of sugar to dry for a few minutes. The sugar should ooze and start to melt. Sprinkle on another layer of icing sugar, then allow to rest for 10 minutes, and bake in the oven at 170°C (gas mark 3 to 4) for 10 to 12 minutes, according to your oven.

Caution: don't open the oven while the biscuits are baking.

You can sandwich these ladyfingers together with a filling of jam or cream, but they are just as delicious served plain.

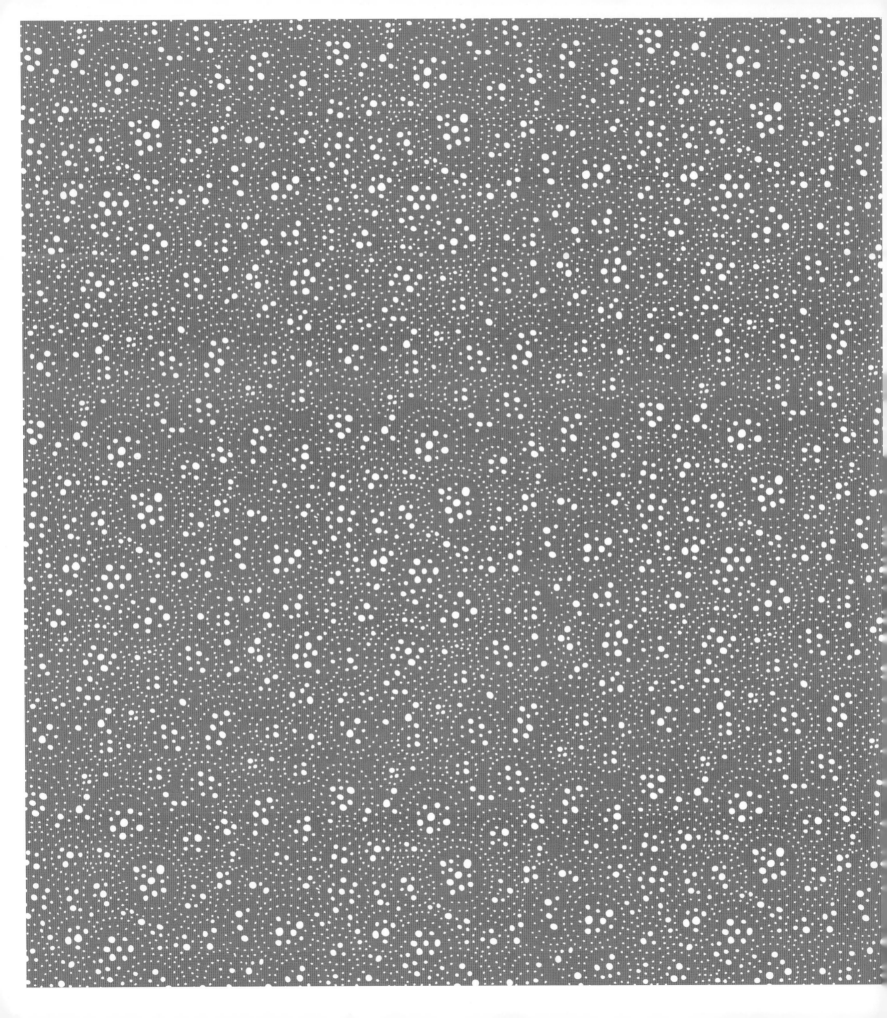

THE CLASSICS

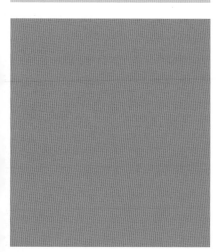

Saint-Honoré

For 6 to 8 people
Preparation time: 1hour 20mins
Cooking time: 1hour
Infusion time: 15mins

100g puff pastry (see page 209)
Icing sugar
Flour, for the work surface
800g choux pastry (see page 210)
300g crème pâtissière (see page 211)

FOR THE STREUSEL PASTRY
40g cold butter
50g flour (+ a bit for the work surface)
50g brown sugar (cassonade, see page 201)
1 pinch fleur de sel

FOR THE CRÈME LÉGÈRE (LIGHT CREAM)
1 gelatin sheet (2g)
120ml single cream
25g mascarpone
10g icing sugar

FOR THE CARAMEL
80g sugar
2 tablespoons water

FOR THE CARAMELISED PUFF PASTRY
Preheat the oven to 170°C (gas mark 3 to 4). Roll out the puff pastry on the floured work surface to make a 20 x 12cm rectangle. Bake for about 15 minutes between two baking trays and two sheets of baking parchment. Remove the top tray and sheet of baking parchment. Sprinkle the pastry generously with icing sugar, using a fine-mesh sieve to sprinkle evenly, and bake for 10 minutes at 230°C (gas mark 8) until caramelised. Keep an eye on the caramelising puff pastry to make sure it doesn't burn.

FOR THE STREUSEL PASTRY
Take the butter out of the fridge 30 minutes before starting the recipe. Combine the flour, brown sugar and the fleur de sel in the bowl of an electric mixer. Knead with the paddle (the flat beater attachment), then add the softened butter. Continue on medium speed to obtain a dough that binds together.
Roll out the pastry on the floured work surface to about 2mm thick. Cut out 12 rounds 1.5cm in diameter using a pastry cutter or a small glass to guide you. Then cut out 3 lengths of pastry 16cm long by 1cm wide and 2mm thick. Place the rounds and strips of pastry between two sheets of baking parchment and put them in the fridge.

FOR THE CHOUX PASTRY (SEE PAGE 210)

BAKE THE CHOUX PASTRY
Preheat the oven to 170°C (gas mark 3 to 4). Fill a piping bag fitted with a plain nozzle with the choux pastry. On a baking tray lined with a sheet of baking parchment, pipe 12 choux buns 3cm in diameter. Use the rest of the pastry to pipe 3 choux sausage shapes about 1cm in diameter and 16cm long. Lay the matching rounds and pieces of streusel on the choux buns and 'sausages'. Bake for 25 minutes and allow to cool at room temperature.

FOR THE CRÈME PÂTISSIÈRE (SEE PAGE 211)

FOR THE CRÈME LÉGÈRE
Soften the gelatin sheet in cold water and squeeze it out thoroughly then add it to the crème pâtissière. Allow the cream to cool and whisk to loosen it.
In the bowl of an electric mixer, whisk up the single cream with the mascarpone and icing sugar at high speed. Then, when the cream has frothed up but is still pliable, incorporate it delicately into the crème pâtissière using a spatula or a whisk.

FOR THE CARAMEL
Put the sugar and water into a saucepan over a medium heat. When the mixture turns a dark copper colour, take the pan off the heat and sit the base in cold water.

TO ASSEMBLE THE CAKE
Using a piping bag, fill the choux buns and sausages (from underneath) with the vanilla cream. Otherwise, cut the buns in half and use a knife and a teaspoon to fill them.
Dip the top of the choux buns in the caramel to give them a smooth, even coating.
Do the same with the 3 choux sausages. Immediately, lay two choux sausages along the long sides of the puff pastry rectangles then a third in the centre, placing each one caramel-side down to stick them in place. Dip the base of the choux buns in the hot caramel then stick them on the two choux sausages laid along the sides.
Generously fill the two spaces between the three sausages with vanilla cream and pipe a light covering over the sausage down the middle as well. Finally, top everything with the vanilla cream, piping any shape you fancy with a fluted nozzle, up to the height of the choux buns.

Religious Dreams

For 6 or 7 people
Preparation time: 1hour
Cooking time: 25mins

FOR THE CHOUX PASTRY

125ml water

125ml semi-skimmed milk

110g butter

5 eggs

140g flour

1 heaped teaspoon caster sugar

1 level teaspoon table salt

FOR THE STREUSEL PASTRY

40g cold butter

50g brown sugar (cassonade, see page 201)

50g flour (+ a bit for the work surface)

1 pinch fleur de sel

FOR THE COFFEE AND CHO-COLATE CRÈME PÂTISSIÈRE

400ml semi-skimmed milk

25g ground coffee (Arabica)

50g egg yolks

60g brown sugar

15g cornflour

10g flour

50g chocolate

30g unsalted butter

2 pinches fleur de sel

FOR THE ITALIAN MERINGUE

100g caster sugar

20ml water

2 egg whites (60g)

FOR THE STREUSEL PASTRY (SEE PAGE 112)

Using a pastry cutter or a small glass to guide you, cut out 7 streusel rounds 2cm in diameter, and 7 rounds 4cm in diameter

FOR THE CHOUX PASTRY (SEE PAGE 210)

BAKE THE CHOUX BUNS

Grease a baking tray with butter, oil or a knob of lard and use a piping bag to pipe the 7 small choux buns (the 'heads' – 2cm in diameter) and 7 large buns (the 'bodies' – 4cm in diameter). Place the corresponding sized streusel rounds on the choux buns.

Bake at 170°C (gas mark 3 to 4), giving the small buns about 15 minutes and the large ones 25 minutes. Then allow to cool completely at room temperature.

FOR THE COFFEE AND CHOCOLATE CRÈME PÂTISSIÈRE

In a saucepan, bring the milk to the boil then add the ground coffee and infuse for 5 minutes but no more than that. Strain through a very fine chinois or better still, through a stocking, to obtain the milk without the coffee grounds. Whisk the egg yolks and brown sugar until slightly pale then add the cornflour and flour.

Break up the chocolate and stir the pieces into the infused milk then heat this mixture again on the hob, whisking to help melt the chocolate.

Off the heat, pour the chocolate and coffee milk in two or three batches into the previous mixture, whisking constantly.

COOK THE CRÈME PÂTISSIÈRE

Transfer the mixture to a saucepan and bring it back to the boil over a medium heat, whisking constantly. Cook the cream for about 1 minute, whisking all the time to prevent it sticking to the bottom of the pan. When the cream has thickened up, on the heat, whisk in the cold butter then the fleur de sel.

Pour the hot cream into a mixing bowl and cover with cling film, patting it down on to the surface to prevent a crust forming. Refrigerate.

Just before you use it, give the cream a whisk for 30 seconds to smooth out any lumps.

FOR THE ITALIAN MERINGUE

In a saucepan, heat the caster sugar and water to 121°C (use a thermometer).

When the syrup reaches 110°C, start whisking the egg whites in the bowl of a freestanding mixer on medium speed.

When the whites have frothed up, finish whisking on the third speed. When they are softly peaking (they should not be too stiff), gradually pour the cooked sugar at 121°C over them in a single stream, whisking constantly on medium speed. After 15 minutes, the egg whites should be glossy and pliable, returned to room temperature and peaks should form at the end of the whisk. Use immediately.

TO ASSEMBLE

Use a piping bag to decorate the small and large choux buns. Pipe a knob of Italian meringue on the large buns and stick the small buns on top, gently pressing down on the knob of meringue which will form the 'collar' around the smaller bun.

Spread a bit of meringue over the small buns and scorch them with a blast from a blow torch.

Tarte Tatin

For 6 to 8 people
Preparation time: 40mins
Cooking time: 1hour 30mins
Refrigeration time: 1 night

200g puff pastry (see page 209)
6 Golden Delicious apples
100g nutty streusel (see page 212)
10g butter, for the tin
Flour for the tin and work surface

FOR THE CARAMEL
80g sugar
2 tablespoons water

FOR THE SYRUP
2 vanilla pods
50ml water
2 tablespoons lemon juice
50g butter
50g sugar
2 pinches fleur de sel

ROLL OUT THE PUFF PASTRY
Roll out the puff pastry to about 5mm thick and use a large, sharp knife to cut out a rectangle 20cm long by 10cm wide. Lay the pastry on a dish and prick it with a fork. Cover with cling film so that the film is touching the pastry and refrigerate for 1 hour.

FOR THE CARAMEL
Pour the sugar and water into a saucepan set over a medium heat. When the mixture turns a dark copper colour, take it off the heat and immediately pour the caramel into a high-sided Teflon® loaf tin, 18cm long by 8cm wide. Tilt it slightly to left and right for the caramel to coat the bottom of the tin.

FOR THE SYRUP
Split the vanilla pods in two, scrape them out and reserve the seeds. In a saucepan set over a medium heat, put the water, lemon juice, butter, sugar, vanilla seeds and the fleur de sel. Blitz with a hand-held electric mixer. Bring to the boil and take off the heat.

COOK THE APPLES
Preheat the oven to 170°C (gas mark 3 to 4). Peel the apples. Use a corer to core then slice them finely into slices 2mm thick using a mandolin. Place the apple slices in the caramelised tin, arranging them in layers up to ²/3 the height of the tin. Drizzle with ²/3 of the syrup prepared above and bake in the oven for about 55 minutes.

When the Tatin apples are cooked, place a weight on top (as you would for foie gras) then allow to cool in the tin at room temperature. When the apples are cold, cover them with cling film and refrigerate until next day.

THE SAME DAY
Give the rectangle of puff pastry a first bake between two sheets of baking parchment and two baking trays to stop it puffing up too much, for about 15 to 17 minutes in a preheated oven at 170 °C (gas mark 3 to 4). Then turn up the oven to 240°C (gas mark 9), sprinkle the pre-cooked rectangle with icing sugar and return it to the oven for the puff pastry to glaze (i.e., for the icing sugar to melt).
To assemble the Tarte Tatin, preheat the oven to 220°C (gas mark 7), take the cling film off the cold Tatin apples and put them in the oven for 2 to 3 minutes so they can be turned out of the tin.

JUST BEFORE SERVING
Using a cloth folded in 4 and both your hands, delicately invert the tin of apples over the puff pastry; the apples will have come unstuck from the sides of the tin and gently fall out.
Your Tarte Tatin is ready to serve at room temperature. You can then decorate the edges of the Tatin with little pieces of streusel (see recipe page 118)

Paris-Brest

For 6 people
Preparation time: 1hour 20mins
Cooking time: 50mins
Refrigeration time: 1hour 30mins

FOR THE STREUSEL PASTRY

50g type 45 flour

50g brown sugar (cassonade, see page 201)

1 pinch fleur de sel

40g cold butter, taken out of the fridge 30 minutes beforehand

FOR THE CHOUX PASTRY

125ml semi-skimmed milk

125ml water

110g cold butter, cut into pieces

140g flour

1 heaped teaspoon caster sugar

1 level teaspoon table salt

5 whole eggs

FOR THE PRALINE CREAM

155ml semi-skimmed milk

2 egg yolks

30g caster sugar

15g cornflour

1 sheet gelatine (2g) soaked in cold water and squeezed

70g unsalted butter, chilled and cut into pieces

80g praliné noisette (shop bought chocolate and hazelnut spread)

FOR DECORATION

Icing sugar

FOR THE STREUSEL PASTRY

In the bowl of an electric mixer, combine the flour, sugar and fleur de sel. Knead with the paddle attachment then add the creamed butter. Continue on medium speed until the butter adheres to the dry ingredients to form a dough. Roll out the pastry between two sheets of baking parchment to about 2mm thick then put it in the fridge. Use a pastry cutter or a small glass to cut out eight rounds of pastry, 3cm in diameter.

FOR THE CHOUX PASTRY (SEE PAGE 210)

Pour the milk and water into a saucepan then the butter cut into pieces. Bring to the boil then tip in the sifted flour, salt and sugar in one go. Stir carefully: a dough will form immediately. Continue stirring over a medium heat for 1 minute to eliminate as much liquid as possible. Then pour the mixture into the bowl of an electric mixer and knead with the paddle attachment, incorporating the whole eggs one at a time. You should obtain a pliable, glossy choux pastry. To check whether the pastry is ready, score a deep line through the surface with your finger for a few centimetres: the groove should close up very slowly. If the choux pastry isn't moist enough, add beaten egg (yolk and white), a little at a time. On a greased baking tray, use a piping bag to pipe eight balls of pastry 4cm in diameter inside a 16cm cake ring, starting with the four cardinal points, then the intermediate quarters: the choux buns should form a crown. Lay the eight rounds of streusel pastry on each of the eight choux buns. Put the crown in the oven at 170°C (gas mark 3 to 4) for 45 minutes then allow to cool at room temperature.

FOR THE PRALINE CREAM

In a saucepan, bring the milk to the boil then take it straight off the heat. In a mixing bowl, whisk together the egg yolks and sugar until pale then add the cornflour. Mix well to obtain a smooth paste then pour in half the milk while still hot. Mix again then pour it all into the pan of milk. Bring the cream to the boil for 1 minute, whisking constantly. When the cream is quite thick, take it off the heat. Add the melted sheet of gelatin to the cream and the almond and hazelnut praline then the chilled butter. Combine everything thoroughly then whizz with a hand-held mixer for a smoother cream. Pour it into a gratin dish for the mixture to spread out and cool more quickly. Cover with cling film, patting it down on to the surface of the cream then set aside in the fridge for 1 hour. When the cream is completely cold, put it in the bowl of an electric mixer and whisk on medium speed for 3 minutes.

TO ASSEMBLE THE PARIS-BREST

When the choux crown is at room temperature, cut it horizontally through the middle. Use a piping bag or tablespoon to place eight generous mounds of praline cream on the eight halved buns in the choux crown. To finish, replace the top of the choux crown and sprinkle with icing sugar to decorate.

FOR THE PRALINE FILLING (OPTIONAL)

Get hold of the praline (from one of the Pâtisseries des Rêves, or using the recipe on page 216) and pour it into the cups of a flexible bun tray then put the tray in the freezer. When you assemble the Paris-Brest, put the frozen half-spheres of praline in the middle of the mounds of praline cream, making sure that they are fully sealed in. When you serve the cake, the praline will be runny.

Rum Babas

For 6 people
Preparation time: 40mins
Resting time: 2hours 30mins
Cooking time: 1hour

FOR THE BABA DOUGH

50g chilled butter cut into chunks

12g fresh yeast

350ml semi-skimmed milk

225g flour

20g sugar

1 level teaspoon fleur de sel

3 eggs

FOR THE SYRUP

900ml water

270ml dark rum

400g caster sugar

1 vanilla pod

FOR THE DOUGH

Take the butter out of the fridge and allow to stand at room temperature for 3 hours. Crumble the yeast into the warmed milk straight into the bowl of an electric mixer then pour over the flour, sugar and fleur de sel. Start to knead the dough at low speed using the dough hook. Incorporate the whole eggs one at a time, lightly beating them first to make the dough as elastic as possible. Continue kneading but on medium speed, making sure that it gradually comes away from the sides of the bowl. This process will take at least 7 minutes. Now gradually add in the butter chunks and knead again for 3 to 4 minutes until the dough comes away from the sides of the bowl again. It should be smooth, homogenous and elastic.

FILL THE MOULDS

Pour the dough into a piping bag fitted with a plain nozzle and fill flexible baba tins (Flexipan®) or savarin moulds. Use kitchen scissors to cut off the dough, which should be very stretchy when it comes out of the piping bag. Smooth the top with your fingers. If you don't have a piping bag, you can perform this operation by simply shaping the dough with your fingers. Place the babas on a baking tray and cover them with cling film, gently and without squashing them, then allow to rise at room temperature (22°C to 24°C, if possible) for about 2 hours. They should be about 75% bigger.

TO BAKE

Preheat the oven to 170°C (gas mark 3 to 4). Bake the babas for 30 minutes, then take them out of the oven (caution: they will be very hot) and put them back in their tins. Return them to the oven for another 30 minutes but at 160°C (gas mark 3) for them to dry out and harden. Allow to cool at room temperature.

FOR THE SYRUP

When the babas are cold, place all the ingredients for the syrup in a large high-sided saucepan and bring to the boil for 30 seconds at most. Wait 2 minutes (because the syrup should not be boiling, just very hot) and immerse the dry babas in the syrup, starting with the base then, when they start to sink and swell up, turn them over with a slotted spoon.

Press them down into the syrup so that they soak it up uniformly. Allow to double in size then take them out with the slotted spoon and arrange on a wire rack placed over the roasting tin from your oven to catch the surplus syrup.

Allow the babas to drain for 2 minutes before arranging them in a dish with a little syrup around the base and cling film over the top. Store in the fridge until serving.

Take them out 20 minutes before serving.

Chocolate Gâteau

For 8 people
Preparation time: 50mins
Cooking time: 35mins
Refrigeration time: 1hour

FOR THE CHOCOLATE
 SPONGE

40g dark chocolate
20g milk chocolate
70g butter (+ for the tin)
90g brown sugar
40g flour (+ for the tin)
½ teaspoon baking powder
90g ground hazelnuts
20g icing sugar
1 generous pinch fleur de sel
1 egg
1 egg yolk
3 egg whites (90g)

FOR THE CHOCOLATE
 GANACHE

140ml semi-skimmed milk
170g dark chocolate
55g milk chocolate

FOR THE SPONGE

Break up the dark and milk chocolate into chunks. Dice the butter. Melt the dark chocolate, the milk chocolate and the butter in a bain-marie. Stir evenly.

In a mixing bowl, use an electric beater to whisk the egg whites and 15g of the brown sugar to frothy peaks that are not too stiff.

Sift the flour and baking powder. Combine the ground hazelnuts, the remaining brown sugar, the icing sugar and the salt. Add in the whole egg and the yolk and whisk for 30 seconds. Add the melted chocolate then the sifted flour and baking powder in two batches. Now incorporate the egg whites half at a time to obtain a pliable, airy dough.

TO BAKE

Preheat the oven to 160°C (gas mark 3). Pour the mixture into a buttered and floured cake ring (16 to 18cm in diameter and 4cm high) placed on a baking tray lined with baking parchment.

If you don't have a cake ring, use a loaf tin or a loose-base sandwich tin. Bake for 20 to 25 minutes. Check to see whether the cake is done by inserting the blade of a knife, which should come out clean. If it doesn't, continue cooking for 5 minutes. At the end of the cooking time, allow the sponge to cool at room temperature then cut it horizontally in two.

FOR THE GANACHE

Heat 120ml of the milk. Take it off the heat just before it boils. Melt the chunks of both chocolates (dark and milk) in a bain-marie. Add the hot milk and whisk to obtain a smooth, glossy ganache.

ASSEMBLE THE GÂTEAU

Use a spatula (or the back of a tablespoon) to spread a third of the ganache over the halved sponge base. Cover with the other half and refrigerate for 15 minutes.

FOR THE ICING

Mix the remaining milk into the rest of the ganache. Whisk for 1 or 2 minutes to obtain a fluid, smooth and glossy ganache.

Put the chilled chocolate cake on a wire rack on the roasting tin of your oven. Pour the chocolate icing generously over the cake to cover it completely, including the sides. Tap the wire rack gently to remove the excess icing and put the cake in the fridge, taking it out 45 minutes before serving.

Salambos

For 6 to 7 people
Preparation time: 1hour
Cooking time: 50mins

FOR THE CHOUX PASTRY
125ml water
125ml semi-skimmed milk
110g butter
5 eggs
140g flour
1 heaped teaspoon caster sugar
1 level teaspoon table salt

FOR THE RUM CRÈME PÂTIS-SIÈRE
500ml semi-skimmed milk
1 vanilla pod
4 egg yolks
85g caster sugar
25g cornflour
20g flour
50g unsalted butter
1.5 sheets gelatin (3g)
40ml dark rum
30ml single cream (35% fat)

FOR THE CARAMEL
240g caster sugar
70g glucose
60ml water

FOR THE CHOUX PASTRY (SEE PAGE 210)

BAKE THE CHOUX BUNS
Using a piping bag, pipe quite large oval choux buns on to a greased baking tray (with butter, oil or a knob of lard).
Bake in the oven at 170°C (gas mark 3 to 4) for 25 to 30 minutes according to your oven.
Allow to cool completely at room temperature.

FOR THE RUM CRÈME PÂTISSIÈRE
In a saucepan, bring the milk to the boil with the split and scraped vanilla pod. Whisk the egg yolks and sugar until pale then add the cornflour and flour.
Off the heat, pour the vanilla-milk over this mixture a half or third at a time, continuing to whisk vigorously.
Transfer the mixture to a saucepan and bring it back to the boil over a medium heat, whisking constantly. Cook the cream for about 1 minute, whisking all the time to prevent it sticking to the bottom of the pan. Soak the gelatin in cold water and squeeze out the excess water. When the cream has thickened up, on the heat, briskly whisk in the cold butter and then the gelatin.
Allow to cool, stirring from time to time then incorporate the rum.

PUT THE CRÈME PÂTISSIÈRE IN THE FRIDGE
Pour the cream into a mixing bowl and cover with cling film, patting it down on to the surface to prevent a crust forming. Put it in the fridge. When you come to use the crème pâtissère, whisk it until smooth then whip up the single cream to chantilly and carefully stir it into the crème pâtissière. Before making the caramel, fill the choux buns with cream using a piping bag.

FOR THE CARAMEL
Start by greasing a sheet of baking parchment spread out on the work surface.
Heat the sugar, glucose and water in a saucepan over a medium heat. As soon as the mixture turns a dark copper colour, take the pan off the heat and stand the base in cold water to stop the cooking process. Put the pan beside the greased sheet of baking parchment.

ICE THE SALAMBOS
Taking care not to burn yourself, dip the top of the choux buns in the caramel (use kitchen tongs if you have any) then turn the buns over and stand them, caramel-side down, on the baking parchment to cool. Turn them over again and if you like, sprinkle them with a little icing sugar.

Cherry Clafoutis

For 8 people
Preparation time: 25mins
Resting time: 15mins
Cooking time: 1hour

500g cherries
135g brown sugar (+ for the tin
    and to sprinkle over the clafou-
    tis before cooking)
3 vanilla pods
3 eggs
70g ground hazelnuts
55g flour
½ level teaspoon fleur de sel
1 heaped teaspoon ground cin-
    namon
25g thick crème fraîche
140ml semi-skimmed milk
Zest of 1 large organic orange
2 tablespoons kirsch (optional)
15g butter, for the tin

FOR THE CRUMBLE
70g creamed butter (take it out
    several hours in advance so
    that the butter is very soft)
30g brown sugar
100g Speculoos (often sold as
    Biskoff Cookies, Belgian Spice
    or Dutch Windmill Cookies)

FOR THE CRUMBLE
Preheat the oven to 160°C (gas mark 3). In a mixing bowl, knead the butter, sugar and crushed Speculoos to make a sweet shortcrust pastry (pâte sablée). Place the pastry on a baking tray lined with baking parchment and flatten it with the palm of your hand to about 5mm thick. Bake in the oven for about 15 to 20 minutes.

FOR THE CHERRIES
Wash the cherries, remove the stalks and drain. Don't take out the stones. Generously butter the baking dish and sprinkle it with brown sugar. Arrange the cherries in it.

FOR THE CLAFOUTIS BATTER
Split and scrape the vanilla pods and reserve the seeds. Use an electric mixer to whisk the eggs until fluffy. Add the ground hazelnuts, vanilla seeds, the brown sugar, flour, fleur de sel, cinnamon, crème fraîche, milk, the orange zest and the kirsch. Blitz with a hand-held mixer to a smooth consistency. Allow to rest for 15 minutes.

TO BAKE
Preheat the oven to 180°C (gas mark 4). Pour the clafoutis batter over the cherries, cover with the coarsely crumbled Speculoos crumble, then sprinkle with brown sugar. Bake for 35 to 40 minutes until the clafoutis is golden brown. Serve at room temperature.

SEASONAL FRUIT TARTS

Rhubarb Tart

300g rhubarb paste
(see page 174)
200g pâte sucrée (see page 208)
Flour, for the work surface
Butter, for the tin

FOR THE ALMOND BUTTER
40g softened butter
20g ground almonds
35g crème pâtissière
(see page 211)
40g icing sugar
10ml rum

FOR THE RHUBARB SLICES
2 stalks fresh rhubarb
Caster sugar

FOR THE RHUBARB PASTRY
The day before: make the rhubarb paste (see page 174) and allow to drain overnight in a fine-mesh sieve.

ROLL OUT THE PASTRY
Roll out the pastry on the floured work surface to about 5mm thick. Line a buttered flan tin with it and place the tin in the fridge for about 2 hours.

TO BAKE BLIND
Preheat the oven to 170°C (gas mark 3 to 4). Take the tin out of the fridge and lay a sheet of baking parchment over the pastry. Fill the case with dried pulses or baking beans and bake for 15 to 20 minutes to lightly colour the pastry. Remove the paper and dried pulses (or baking beans). Turn the oven down to 150°C (gas mark 2).

FOR THE ALMOND BUTTER
In a mixing bowl, whisk together the softened butter and ground almonds. Add the crème pâtissière, icing sugar and the rum. Whisk to obtain a homogenous mixture.

FILL THE PASTRY CASE
Spread the almond butter over the pastry case to about 5mm thick and to within 1cm of the edge. Bake for 15 to 20 minutes until the almond butter is golden but still soft.

FOR THE RHUBARB SLICES
Strip the rhubarb stalks then cut each one lengthwise into 3 equal lengths. Take a sharp knife and cut along each length again to obtain about 20 slices ½cm thick.
Lay the rhubarb slices flat on a baking tray lined with a sheet of baking parchment then sprinkle generously with caster sugar. Bake at 150°C (gas mark 2) for 3 to 4 minutes at most until lightly caramelised.

TO FINISH
Lastly, fill the case with the rhubarb paste up to the top of the tin. Smooth over the surface then arrange the caramelised rhubarb slices on top, laying them side by side before serving.

Tangy Strawberry Tart

For 6 to 8 people
Preparation time: 45mins
Refrigeration time: 14hours
Cooking time: 30mins

100g rhubarb paste
   (see page 174)
200g pâte sucrée (see page 208)
100g almond butter
   (see page 132)
20g medium-sized Gariguette
   strawberries
50g candied soft fruit (see below)
Flour, for the work surface
Butter, for the tin

**FOR THE CANDIED SOFT
   FRUIT**
(minimum quantity you can make)
90g strawberries
25g raspberries
15g redcurrants
10g blackcurrants
60g granulated sugar
2 tablespoons lime juice
25ml lemon juice
Zest of ½ lemon
½ teaspoon pectin (Vitpris®)

**FOR THE RHUBARB PASTE AND CANDIED
SOFT FRUIT**

The day before: make the rhubarb paste (see page
174) and allow to drain overnight in a fine-mesh
sieve.
Now prepare the candied soft fruit by combining
the soft fruit and half the granulated sugar in
a bowl. Pour in the lime juice, lemon juice and
lemon zest. Cover the mixture with cling film then
set aside in the fridge for at least 12 hours.

ROLL OUT THE PASTRY CASE
On the floured work surface, roll out the biscuit
pastry to 5mm thick. Use the rolling pin to help
you lay it in a buttered flan tin. Press the pastry
lightly into the base and edges of the tin with your
thumbs. Refrigerate for 2 hours.

PRE-COOK THE PASTRY
Preheat the oven to 170°C (gas mark 3 to 4).
Take the case out of the fridge and lay a sheet of
baking parchment over the pastry. Fill the case
with dried pulses (large beans) or baking beans to
stop the pastry puffing up, and bake for 15 to 20
minutes to lightly colour the pastry.

SPREAD THE ALMOND BUTTER
Spread the almond butter over the blind-baked
pastry case to 5mm thick and to within 1cm of the
edge. Bake for another 5 minutes at 150°C (gas
mark 2) until the almond butter is golden but still
soft.

PREPARE THE STRAWBERRIES
Wash the strawberries, remove the stalks and drain.
Cut them in half from top to bottom.

FOR THE CANDIED SOFT FRUIT
Combine the pectin with the remaining sugar. In
a saucepan over a medium heat (about 40°C),
cook the macerated fruit in their juice then add
the mixture of pectin and sugar. Bring to the boil
for 30 seconds, pour the candied soft fruit into a
mixing bowl then place cling film directly over the
surface and put the fruit in the fridge.

TO FINISH THE TART
Cover the tart base with the rhubarb paste to 1cm
thick, smooth the paste evenly, spread 50g candied
soft fruit over it then lay the strawberry halves on
top. Working outwards from the centre, arrange
them in concentric circles with the flat side of the
fruit underneath.

Apple Tartlets

For 4 people
Preparation time: 40mins
Refrigeration time: 2hours
Cooking time: 25mins

400g puff pastry (see page 209)
   or 2 rolls of ready-made pastry
6 Golden Delicious apples
20g caster sugar
120g almond butter (see page
   132)
40g lightly salted butter
4 tablespoons brown sugar
Fleur de sel
Flour, for the work surface

CUT OUT THE PASTRY CASES
On the floured work surface, roll out the puff pastry to 5mm thick, prick it all over with a fork then cut out 4 rounds of pastry, 14cm in diameter, using a pastry cutter or a plate to guide you. Cover with cling film then allow the pastry rounds to rest in the fridge for at least 2 hours.

FOR THE APPLES
Peel, core and halve the apples from top to bottom. Cut the halves into slices 5mm thick.

FILL THE PASTRY CASES
Take the pastry rounds out of the fridge, lay them on a baking tray lined with well buttered baking parchment and sprinkle with caster sugar. On each round of puff pastry, place a heaped tablespoon of almond butter and spread it to 4mm thick and to within 1cm of the edge.

ARRANGE THE SLICES OF APPLE
Preheat the oven to 160°C (gas mark 3). Arrange the apple slices on the tart bases in five or six layers of overlapping concentric circles. Allow the equivalent of one and a half apples per tart. Now divide up little knobs of chilled, lightly salted butter equally between the tarts and sprinkle with brown sugar and a few grains of fleur de sel.

BAKE THE TARTS
Bake for about 25 minutes. Take the tarts out of the oven and allow to cool on a wire rack before serving.

Quince Tarte Tatin

For 6 people
Preparation time: 35mins
Cooking time: 1hour 40mins
Refrigeration time: 12hours

200g puff pastry (see page 209)
    or 1 roll of ready-made pastry
4 Golden Delicious apples
3 quinces
100g butter
110g caster sugar
1 tablespoon lemon juice
Flour, for the mould and work
    surface

FOR THE SYRUP
500ml water
Juice of ½ lemon
200g brown sugar
2 star anise
1 cinnamon stick
1 vanilla pod

CUT OUT THE PASTRY CASE
On the floured work surface, roll out the puff
pastry to ½cm thick. Use a 20cm cake ring to cut
out a round. Prick the base you obtain with a fork,
lay it between two sheets of baking parchment
and set aside in the fridge.

FOR THE APPLES AND QUINCES
Peel the apples and quinces, cut them in half and
remove the core and pips.

POACH THEM IN SYRUP
In a saucepan over a medium heat, put the water,
lemon juice, brown sugar, star anise, cinnamon and
the split and scraped vanilla pod. Put the fruit in
the pan and cook for 50 minutes until the quinces
are soft right through. Drain the fruit and cut the
ends off the half-quinces so that they more-or-less
match the shape of the apple halves.

CARAMELISE THE FRUIT
Slice the butter and put three quarters of it into
an oven-proof frying pan. Sprinkle with 85g
sugar then arrange the fruit on top in a spiral of
alternating apples and quinces, packing them in
very tightly. Cover the fruit with the remaining
butter and sugar.
Now start to cook over a low heat then, when
the mixture starts to froth up, add the lemon juice.

Heat until caramelisation occurs, turning the
frying pan if necessary to get the same colour all
over. This stage is vital because the reduction and
caramelisation of the butter, sugar and pectin in
the fruit is what gives the tart its characteristic
colour and flavour.

TO BAKE
Preheat the oven to 180°C (gas mark 4). When
you have obtained the desired colour, put the pan
in the oven for 15 minutes until the apples are
fully cooked on top (quinces don't have the same
structure). Take the tart out of the oven and allow
the fruit to cool at room temperature.

FINISH BAKING THE TART
Now put the round of puff pastry over the fruit,
tucking the edges of the pastry in towards the
centre. Return the tart to the oven for 25 minutes
(still at 180°C, gas mark 4).
Allow to cool to room temperature then cover
with cling film and put the tart in the fridge for at
least 12 hours.

TO SERVE THE TART
To turn out the tart, place the frying pan over a
medium heat, stirring gently to unstick the sides
and base, then invert it on to a flat dish. Serve cold
or just warm.

Mango and Pineapple Tart

For 4 to 6 people
Preparation time: 1hour 10mins
Marinade time: 2hours
Cooking time: 2hours 20mins

110g pâte sucrée (see page 208)
1 teaspoon pectin (Vitpris®)
1 mango (about 100g)
1 tablespoon grated coconut

FOR THE PINEAPPLE MARINADE
185g pineapple (fresh or frozen)
1 vanilla pod
1 pinch lime zest
1 teaspoon lime juice
1 teaspoon vanilla extract
4g sugar
1 pinch fleur de sel

FOR THE ALMOND BUTTER
30g butter
30g icing sugar
1 egg yolk
30g ground almonds
1 teaspoon rum
12g crème pâtissière
   (see page 211)

FOR THE COMPOTE
110g pineapple (fresh or frozen)
120ml water
5g brown sugar
1 vanilla pod
50ml lime juice
1 pinch lime zest
1 pinch fleur de sel
½ teaspoon rum

FOR THE COCONUT STREUSEL
65g butter
80g flour
20g ground almonds
40g ground coconut
1 vanilla pod
1g salt

FOR THE MARINATED PINEAPPLE
Cut the pineapple into small cubes or sticks. Split the vanilla pod and scrape out the seeds with a knife. Put the pineapple cubes into a bowl with the finely grated zest and juice of the lime, the vanilla extract and the sugar, salt and vanilla seeds. Allow to marinate for at least 2 hours.

FOR THE PASTRY CASE
Preheat the oven to 170°C (gas mark 3 to 4). Roll out the pastry and line an 18cm flan tin or ring with it. Line it with baking parchment and baking beans. Bake blind for 25 to 30 minutes to lightly colour the pastry.

FOR THE ALMOND BUTTER
Meanwhile, mix the softened butter, which should be very pliable, with the icing sugar. In order and stirring each ingredient thoroughly as you add it, incorporate the egg yolk, the ground almonds, the rum and the crème pâtissière. Spread this mixture over the tart base and bake for another 15 minutes.

FOR THE COMPOTE
Place the pineapple chunks, 120ml water and the brown sugar in a saucepan with the split and scraped vanilla pod. Cook for 10 minutes over a medium heat, mixing evenly. Reduce the heat and continue cooking for 10 minutes. Now add the lime juice and finely grated zest, the fleur de sel and the rum. Cook for 10 minutes. Allow to cool.

FOR THE STREUSEL
Use your fingertips to rub all the ingredients together to a sandy consistency like a crumble with fairly big lumps. Tip the streusel on to a baking tray lined with baking parchment and bake for 35 to 40 minutes at 140°C (gas mark 1) until it starts to colour.

CATCH AND THICKEN THE JUICE FROM THE MARINADE
Drain the marinated pineapple. Catch the juice and measure out about 200ml. Boil the juice with the pectin for 30 seconds. Stir into the drained pineapple chunks.

TO FINISH THE TART
Spread the compote over the base of the tart. Peel the mango, cut it in two around the stone then slice it finely into 3 or 4 slices. Smooth the surface of the tart with a spatula.
Lay the mango slices on the compote, cutting them up and arranging them like the pieces of a jigsaw puzzle so that they cover the whole surface. Divide up the pineapple chunks on top, smooth the surface with a spatula and bake for the last time at 170°C (gas mark 3 to 4) for 15 minutes. Take the tart out of the oven, allow to cool and sprinkle the top with pieces of streusel and grated coconut. Serve chilled.

Pear Tart with Champomy® Caramel

For 4 people
Preparation time: 40mins
Refrigeration time: 2hours
Cooking time: 40mins

200g puff pastry (see page 209)
   or 1 roll of ready-made
   puff pastry
10 large, ripe juicy Comice pears
20g caster sugar
40g slightly salted butter
4 tablespoons brown sugar
   (cassonade, see page 201)
40g unsalted butter
Flour, for the work surface
Fleur de sel

FOR THE COMPOTE
25g butter
30g caster sugar
1 vanilla pod
2 pinches fleur de sel
3 tablespoons pear brandy

FOR THE CHAMPOMY®
   CARAMEL
40ml single cream
30ml semi-skimmed milk
125g caster sugar
70ml Champomy®
Grated zest of ½ organic orange
2 pinches fleur de sel

CUT OUT THE PASTRY CASE

On the floured work surface, roll out the puff pastry to 5mm thick, prick it all over with a fork then cut out 4 rounds of pastry 14cm in diameter using a pastry cutter or a plate to guide you. Cover with cling film then allow the rounds to rest in the fridge for at least 2 hours.

FOR THE PEARS

Peel and core the pears. Cut 2 of them into medium-sized cubes. Cut the remaining pears into slices 5mm thick.

COOK THE COMPOTE

In a saucepan set over a medium heat, melt the butter with the sugar and the split and scraped vanilla pod. Add the pear cubes, the fleur de sel and the pear brandy. Now, cook the pears on a low heat for 6 to 7 minutes, stirring frequently. The aim is to get the moisture to evaporate to reduce the compote and concentrate the flavour. The resulting compote should be quite firm, and all the better if there are still a few lumps in it. Take it off the heat and allow to cool at room temperature then put it in the fridge covered with cling film.

FILL THE PASTRY CASES

Arrange the rounds of pastry on a sheet of baking parchment, brush with butter and sprinkle with caster sugar (shake off the surplus). On each round of puff pastry, lay a heaped tablespoon of pear compote, spreading it to 4mm thick and to within 1cm of the edge.

ADD THE PEAR SLICES

Preheat the oven to 160°C (gas mark 3). Arrange the pear slices in the pastry cases in overlapping concentric circles to make 4 or 5 layers. In each pastry case, you should put the equivalent of 2 pears. Now, divide up knobs of slightly salted butter equally between the tarts and sprinkle with brown sugar and a few grains of fleur de sel.

TO COOK THE TARTS

Place in the oven for about 25 minutes. Take the tarts out of the oven and allow to cool on a wire rack before serving.

FOR THE CHAMPOMY® CARAMEL

In a small saucepan, heat the cream and milk on a low heat. In another pan over a medium heat, melt the sugar stirring constantly with a wooden spoon. When the caramel turns a dark copper colour, gradually pour it in a single stream over the warm cream-and-milk mixture, whisking constantly. When the cream is entirely incorporated, continue cooking the caramel, bringing it to the boil for about 30 seconds. Take it off the heat then add in the Champomy®, the orange zest and the fleur de sel. Blend with a hand-held mixer.

TO SERVE

Arrange the tarts on plates and pour over the Champomy® caramel before serving.

Orange Tart

For 6 people
Preparation time: 55mins
Refrigeration time: 2hours
Cooking time: 7hours

200g pâte sucrée
  (see page 208)
Flour, for the work surface

FOR THE CANDIED ORANGE
3 or 4 organic oranges
75g sugar

FOR THE ORANGE CREAM
2 or 3 organic oranges
2 sheets gelatin (4g)
4 eggs
95g sugar
105g butter (+ a little for the tin)

We can't give you the exact recipe for the orange tart icing, because it is made from ingredients that are hard to get hold of, such as neutral Harmony coating, food colouring for professionals, orange purée and crystal syrup or yellow pectin NH.
However, Philippe Conticini suggests a substitute: some specialist shops sell powdered food colouring. Take an orange food colouring or a mix of red and lemon yellow. Buy the powdered glazing for tarts and follow the manufacturer's instructions to reconstitute it, adding the powdered colourings and 10% more water than the weight initially recommended. To ice the tart (normally spray-glazed), you can use a small ladle as you would to ice a chocolate cake. Your icing should be runny but above all not too hot so as not to melt the cream (maximum temperature, 40°C).

ROLL OUT THE PASTRY CASE
On the floured work surface, roll out the puff pastry to 5mm thick. Line a buttered flan tin with it and refrigerate for about 2 hours.

TO BAKE BLIND
Preheat the oven to 170°C (gas mark 3 to 4). Take the tin out of the fridge, cover the pastry with a sheet of baking parchment and fill the case with dried pulses or baking beans and bake for 15 to 20 minutes to lightly colour the pastry. Remove the paper and dried pulses (or baking beans).

FOR THE CANDIED ORANGE
Wash the oranges and remove the peel leaving as little of the white pith as possible. Squeeze the oranges and reserve the juice. Weigh out 50g peel and measure out 125ml of the juice.
Put the orange peel in a saucepan, pour in enough cold water to cover and bring to the boil. Empty the saucepan through a sieve and retain the peel. Return the peel to the pan and repeat the process twice more.

FOR THE CANDIED PEEL
Put the blanched peel back in the pan and pour in the orange juice and sugar. Cook on a low heat for about 40 to 50 minutes. Blend the mixture.

FOR THE ORANGE CREAM
Soften the gelatin in a bowl of cold water. Take the zest of 1 orange and slice it finely. Squeeze the juice from the oranges. Strain 120ml of the juice and heat it in a saucepan over a medium heat with the orange zests, without letting it boil. In a mixing bowl, whisk the eggs with the sugar until pale then add half the candied orange and the hot orange juice. Whisk vigorously then pour the mixture into a saucepan. Cook the cream on a low heat, whisking constantly, and bring it almost to boiling point without letting it boil. When the cream is thick and cooked, take it off the heat and stir in the drained gelatin and the chilled diced butter. Whisk the mixture vigorously then blend with a hand-held mixer to obtain an even smoother, creamier consistency. Pour the cream into a gratin dish for it to spread out and cool more quickly. Cover with cling film, patting it down on to the cream then put it in the fridge for at least 3 hours.

TO ASSEMBLE THE TART
Spread the remaining candied orange over the baked pastry case then pour over the cream to form a dome. Refrigerate for 2 hours before serving.

Banana and Coffee Tart

For 6 to 7 people
Preparation time: 10mins
Refrigeration time: 2hours
Cooking time: 30 to 40mins

200g pâte sucrée (see page 208)
4 or 5 ripe bananas (depending
   on size)
20g butter (+ for the tin)
2 tablespoons brown sugar
Juice of ½ lemon
1 vanilla pod
2 pinches fleur de sel
1 sprig lemon thyme

FOR THE ALMOND AND COFFEE BUTTER
20g ground almonds
40g butter
2 heaped tablespoons crème
   pâtissière (see page 211)
40g icing sugar
1 tablespoon rum
1 slightly heaped tablespoon instant coffee

FOR THE STREUSEL
50g slightly salted butter
50g type 45 flour
50g brown sugar (cassonade,
   see page 201)
65g ground hazelnuts
2 pinches fleur de sel

FOR THE PASTRY CASE
Roll out the pastry to ½cm thick then, using a rolling pin to help you, carefully line a lightly buttered ring or flan tin with it, gently pressing it into the edges with your thumbs. Bake the pastry case at 170°C (gas mark 3 to 4) for 15 to 20 minutes, depending on your oven, until the pastry is a light golden colour.

FOR THE ALMOND BUTTER WITH COFFEE
In a mixing bowl, whisk together the ground almonds and softened butter. Add the crème pâtissière, icing sugar, the rum and the instant coffee. Whisk again to obtain a smooth cream.

FOR THE STREUSEL
Take the butter out of the fridge 30 minutes beforehand. In another bowl, mix together the dry ingredients (flour, brown sugar, salt and ground hazelnuts) then add the slightly salted butter cut into chunks. Knead with your hands until the butter binds with the dry ingredients but doesn't yet form a dough. The mixture should resemble a crumble topping. Spread it over a tray lined with baking parchment and bake for about 15 to 20 minutes at 160°C (gas mark 3).

FRY THE BANANAS
Remove the skins and cut the bananas into slanting slices 1.5cm thick. In a frying pan, heat the butter over a low heat till foaming and add the brown sugar then the lemon juice. Mix with a spatula, stir in the seeds from the vanilla pod and the fleur de sel then simmer for 10 seconds and pour the mixture over the bananas. Add the lemon thyme sprig and stir gently so that the bananas soak up this aromatic juice. Allow to cool at room temperature.

FILL THE PASTY CASE
Spread the tart base with the coffee-and-almond butter to a good ½cm thick. Arrange circles of the slanting banana slices on top and finish with a sprinkle of the streusel.
If you like, you can decorate it with icing sugar.

Blueberry and Almond Tart

For 6 to 7 people
Preparation time: 1hour 15mins
Refrigeration time: 3hour 45mins
Cooking time: 45mins

200g pâte sucrée (see page 208)

FOR THE ALMOND BUTTER
20g ground almonds
40g creamed butter
35g crème pâtissière
  (see page 211)
40g icing sugar
10ml rum
200g ground caramelised nuts
  (see page 215)

FOR THE BLUEBERRY
  FILLING
60g frozen blueberries
15g caster sugar
140ml crème de cassis
3 level teaspoons cornflour
2 teaspoons water
2 sheets gelatine (4g)
Juice of 1 large lemon
175g fresh blueberries

FOR THE ALMOND CREAM
180g vanilla crème pâtissière
  (see page 211)
40g marzipan
25g butter
10g cocoa butter
3 sheets gelatin (6g)
2 tablespoons rum

FOR THE PÂTE SUCRÉE (SEE PAGE 208)

FOR THE ALMOND BUTTER
In a mixing bowl, whisk together the ground almonds with the creamed butter (take it out of the fridge an hour beforehand). Add the crème pâtissière, the icing sugar and the rum. Whisk everything again to obtain a smooth cream. Fill the pre-cooked pastry case with this almond butter to a good ½cm thick and smooth it to within 1cm of the edge. Put the tart back in the oven at 150°C (gas mark 2) until the almond butter is golden but is still soft.

STRAIN THE BLUEBERRY JUICE
In a mixing bowl, mix together the frozen blueberries and the sugar.
Cover with cling film then heat the berries in the microwave on full power for 1 minute.
Strain the blueberry juice through a chinois.

FOR THE BLUEBERRY FILLING
Pour 50ml of the blueberry juice and crème de cassis into a saucepan. Bring to the boil then reduce the liquid over a medium heat for 1 minute. Dissolve the cornflour in the 2 teaspoons of cold water then add it a little at a time to the pan to thicken the liquid, still on a medium heat, whisking constantly to obtain a very thick and syrupy juice. Meanwhile soak the gelatin sheets in a bowl of

cold water and squeeze dry then add them to the juice. Allow to cool then pour in the lemon juice. In a mixing bowl, pour the blueberry juice and cassis mixture over the fresh blueberries. Stir carefully to coat the berries all over with the juice then set aside in the fridge.

FOR THE ALMOND CREAM
In the bowl of an electric mixer, combine the vanilla crème pâtissière (the kind used for cream choux buns) and the marzipan. Whisk on medium speed to obtain a smooth, homogenous cream. Incorporate the butter and cocoa butter (melt them first) then mix thoroughly. Soak the gelatin sheets in a bowl of water and squeeze dry then melt them in the microwave for a few seconds. Add them to the almond cream and mix then pour in the rum. Place the mixture in the fridge for 1 hour then whip up the cream again, whisking on medium speed for a few minutes.

TO FINISH THE TART
Line the tart base with almond butter, cover with a layer of the blueberry filling adding a little of the thick sauce then spread the almond cream on top, smoothing it in a circular motion up into a dome. Finish by scattering finely ground caramelised nuts all over the top of the tart.
Refrigerate for 45 minutes before serving.

FREESTYLE CAKES

Sugared Almond Cake

For 6 or 7 people
Preparation time: 50mins
Freezing time: 2hours
Refrigeration time: 3 to 4hours
Cooking time: 50mins

FOR THE SPONGE BASE

190g marzipan

Zest of 1 lemon

190g whole eggs (4 small eggs), beaten

40g type 55 flour

1 good pinch fleur de sel

½ teaspoon baking powder

60g butter

FOR THE COMPOTE

110g apricot jam

50g dried apricots

45ml lemon juice

1 level teaspoon pectin (Vitpris®)

FOR THE ICING

100ml single cream

½ vanilla pod

20g sugared almonds

100g white chocolate

40g butter

1 drop bitter almond extract (optional)

FOR THE CRÈME PÂTISSIÈRE

110ml semi-skimmed milk

65g sugared almonds (see recipe for crème pâtissière, page 211)

FOR THE MOUSSE

70g Italian meringue (see page 114)

180ml single cream (35 % fat)

45g mascarpone

2.5 sheets gelatine (5g)

1 drop bitter almond extract (optional)

FOR THE SPONGE BASE

Preheat the oven to 170°C (gas mark 3 to 4). Using the paddle attachment of a small freestanding mixer, combine the marzipan with the lemon zest then add the beaten eggs. Beat to an emulsion, increasing the speed until the mixture is light in colour with a ribbon consistency. Now incorporate, half at a time, the flour mixed with the fleur de sel and the baking powder, then melt the butter and gently add it in an even stream. Lay a cake ring on a sheet of baking parchment placed on the baking sheet of your oven and pour in the sponge dough to a depth of 2cm (or use a buttered and floured, 18cm square cake tin or a 20 by 10cm rectangular tin). Bake in the oven for 15 to 20 minutes, according to your oven. The sponge should be golden, pliable and soft. Allow to cool and set aside.

FOR THE APRICOT COMPOTE

In a saucepan over a medium heat, bring the apricot jam to the boil with the diced dried apricots and the lemon juice, whisking constantly. Now add the spoonful of Vitpris®, whisking vigorously all the time, and allow to boil for 20 seconds before taking it off the heat.

FOR THE ICING

In a saucepan, bring the cream to the boil with the whole vanilla pod then tip the sugared almonds in. Infuse for about 10 minutes, blend everything thoroughly and strain through a chinois. Bring the infused cream back to the boil and pour it over the coarsely chopped white chocolate. Whisk vigorously, then add the butter and bitter almond extract. Blend and set aside.

FOR THE CRÈME PÂTISSIÈRE WITH SUGARED ALMONDS

In a saucepan, bring the milk to the boil then tip the sugared almonds in. Infuse for about 10 minutes and blend thoroughly, then strain through a chinois. Use this milk to make the crème pâtissière (see page 211). Place cling film directly over the surface of the crème and allow to cool slowly.

FOR THE MOUSSE

The crème pâtissière should be barely warm for this preparation. Make an Italian meringue (see page 114). Whip up the single cream to chantilly then whisk it into the mascarpone half at a time. Whisk in the soaked and squeezed gelatin sheets. Incorporate into the crème pâtissière, first, the whipped cream with mascarpone half at a time, then carefully add the Italian meringue and bitter almond extract.

TO ASSEMBLE

Place your (clean) ring on a sheet of baking parchment placed on a baking sheet or flat plate. Lay the sponge base at the bottom and trim it so that it is no more than 2cm high with a diameter about 2 or 3mm less. Spread a ½cm layer of apricot compote over the sponge base and pour over it the sugared almond mousse to the same height as the ring. Use a stainless steel palette knife to make sure the mousse fills the 2 to 3mm gap between the ring and the sponge base, and press your knife over the edges of the ring to smooth the top.

FREEZE AND ICE THE CAKE

Put your cake in the freezer for at least 2 hours. Warm the ganache icing very slightly, turn the frozen cake out of the mould by giving the ring a blast with a blowtorch then place it on a wire rack with a large plate or baking parchment underneath to catch anything that falls through the bars of the rack. Place the cake on the rack and pour the warmed icing all over it. Use a palette knife to smooth the icing in a back-and-forth motion. The whole cake should be covered. Put the cake in the fridge, allow to defrost slowly for 3 to 4 hours and take it out just before serving.

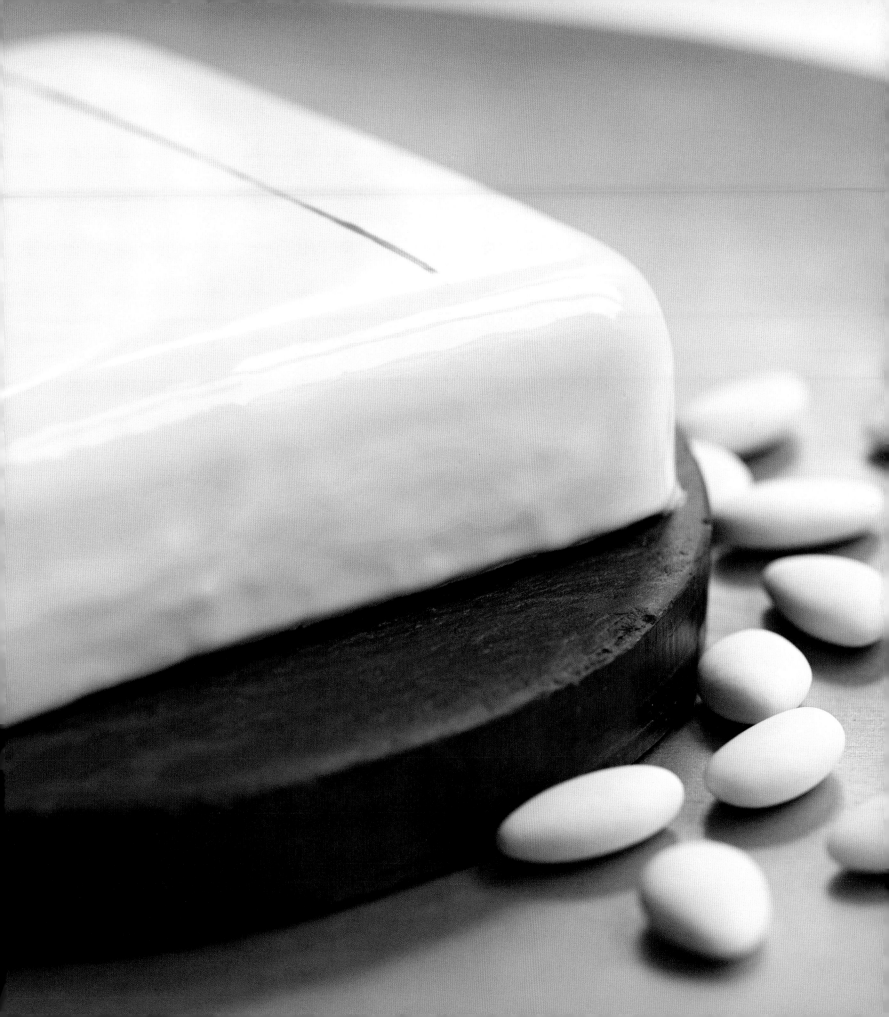

Snow Meringues

For 6 or 7 people
Preparation time: 1hour 20mins
Cooking time: 1hour 30mins
Freezing time: 1hour

FOR THE COATING
10 ladies finger biscuits

FOR THE CITRUS MERINGUES
40g caster sugar
40g egg whites
2 good pinches fleur de sel
Zest of 1 lemon
Zest of ½ lime
40g icing sugar

FOR THE BUTTER CREAM
50ml semi-skimmed milk
15ml single cream
1 vanilla pod
1 egg yolk + 1 egg
45g sugar
200g butter
1 tablespoon mascarpone

FOR THE ITALIAN MERINGUE
1 egg white
50g caster sugar
2 tablespoons water

**FOR THE BLACK SESAME
  CREAM**
160ml single cream
35ml whole milk
½ vanilla pod
40g brown sugar
Zest of 2 small lemons
15g dark chocolate
2 teaspoons black sesame seeds
2.5 sheets gelatin (5g)

TO DECORATE
Icing sugar
Black sesame seeds

FOR THE COATING

Crush then process the biscuits very finely. Sift the powder you obtain through a fine-mesh sieve. Dry it out in a cool oven (100°C) for 3 or 4 hours. Store the coating in a dry place in an airtight box.

FOR THE CITRUS MERINGUE

Place the bowl of a stand mixer over a saucepan of simmering water for a bain-marie and whisk together the caster sugar and egg whites until the mixture is warm/hot (45-50°) Then, put the bowl in the mixer fitted with the whisk and whisk on speed 3 until foamy. At the end, whisk in a pinch of fleur de sel on speed 1 together with the lemon and lime zests. To finish the meringue, sprinkle in the icing sugar and stir it in delicately from top to bottom with a spatula.

Use a piping bag with a plain nozzle to fill silicone half-sphere moulds 6cm in diameter and smooth the top with a palette knife. Cook the meringues in the oven at 100°C (gas mark ¼) for an hour to an hour and a quarter, according to your oven.

FOR THE ITALIAN MERINGUE (SEE PAGE 114)

FOR THE BUTTER CREAM

In a saucepan, bring the milk and the cream to the boil with the split and scraped vanilla pod. Meanwhile, whisk the egg yolk with the whole egg and the sugar until thick and pale. When the vanilla milk boils, pour it over the egg mixture a half or third at a time, whisking vigorously.

Return everything to the pan over a medium heat and stir with a wooden spatula in a figure of eight without stopping. Don't be afraid to take the saucepan off the heat, continuing to stir, if the cream thickens up too fast.

When the cream is done, strain it into the bowl of a small freestanding mixer. To cool it down, give it a whisk in the mixer on speed 2. When the cream is all but cool (about 30°C at most), gradually stir in the chunks of butter at room temperature, then whisk to trap the air bubbles and give the mixture some volume. Whip up the cream to chantilly and stir a third of it into the mascarpone then delicately stir in the remainder with a spatula, mixing delicately from top to bottom. Finally, fold in the Italian meringue.

FOR THE BLACK SESAME CREAM

Heat the cream, the milk, the half vanilla pod split and scraped, the brown sugar and the lemon zests. Take out the vanilla pod then pour in the chopped dark chocolate, whisk vigorously and add the black sesame and the soaked and squeezed gelatin sheets. Allow to cool slightly then half-fill glass tumblers with the cream. Cover with cling film and put the tumblers in the fridge.

TO ASSEMBLE

Use silicone half-sphere moulds 7cm in diameter. Using a spatula, coat each hole with a fairly thin layer of the butter cream (4mm thick). In each coated hole, place a half-sphere citrus meringue shell, spread another thin layer of butter cream over the meringue and smooth over to the top of the moulds to fully enclose the meringue shells and seal any gaps. Place the moulds in the freezer for at least an hour then turn out the half-spheres on to cling film or baking parchment and put them quickly back in the freezer. Take them out to room temperature for 2 minutes before rolling them delicately by hand in the biscuit crumb coating, making sure the crumbs adhere. Carefully place a half-sphere in the middle of each glass on the set cream and scatter with a few grains of black sesame. Put them back in the fridge and serve chilled.

Goats Cheese Tart with Mango and Avocado

For 4 to 6 people
Preparation time: 1hour
Cooking time: 30mins

200g pâte sucrée (see page 208)
1 very ripe mango
4 figs
1 small very ripe avocado
50g streusel (see page 212)
Fleur de sel
A few pinches brown sugar
Flour, for the work surface

FOR THE VANILLA OLIVE OIL
1 vanilla pod
200ml olive oil

FOR THE GOATS CHEESE AND
   MANGO PASTE
120g mango
80g fresh goats cheese
2 sprigs lemon thyme (or 4 fresh
   mint leaves, finely chopped)

BAKE THE PASTRY CASE BLIND
Preheat the oven to 160°C (gas mark 3). Roll out the pastry on the floured work surface and line an 18cm buttered and floured flan tin. Prick the pastry with a fork and bake in the oven for about 25 to 30 minutes to colour slightly.

FOR THE VANILLA OIL
Split the vanilla pod in two, scrape it out and reserve the seeds. Place the pod in a bowl and drizzle the oil over it, whisking to obtain a smooth emulsion.

FOR THE FRUIT
Cut both ends off the mango. Stand it upright on a chopping board and cut away strips of peel working from top to bottom with a knife. Still working from top to bottom, cut slices of mango about 5mm thick, swivelling the fruit round its stone.
Rinse the figs, pat dry and remove the stalks. Crush them with a fork, skin included, to obtain a lumpy purée.
Peel the avocado and cut it into slices about 1cm thick. Arrange them on a dish and use a pastry brush to brush them with vanilla olive oil. Sprinkle them lightly with fleur de sel and more generously with brown sugar.

FOR THE MIXTURE
Dice the mango. Tip the diced mango, the goats cheese and the finely chopped lemon thyme into a shallow dish. Crush everything with a fork to obtain a lumpy purée.

FILL THE PASTRY CASE
Spread two thirds of the mango purée over the pastry case right up to the edge. Similarly but more in the middle, spread the fig purée, leaving a 2cm border all around.
Now add the seasoned avocado slices then spread the remaining mango and goats cheese paste over everything.
Smooth the surface with a spatula, the blade of a large knife or the back of a tablespoon. Now divide up the mango slices and arrange them so that they overlap. Brush with vanilla olive oil then sprinkle with streusel. Decorate with a sprig of lemon thyme before serving.

Coffee Cake

For 6 or 7 people
Preparation time: 1hour 20mins
Refrigeration time: 30mins
Cooking time: 1hour

FOR THE COFFEE SPONGE BASE

85g butter (+ for the mould)
2 teaspoons instant coffee
90g ground hazelnuts
30g icing sugar
90g brown sugar
125g egg whites (4)
30g egg yolks (1.5)
45g type 45 flour (+ a little for the mould)
2 pinches fleur de sel
1 teaspoon baking powder
2 vanilla pods

FOR THE STREUSEL

50g softened slightly salted butter
50g brown sugar (cassonade, see page 201)
65g ground hazelnuts
50g type 45 flour
2 pinches fleur de sel

FOR THE MERINGUE

100g caster sugar
3 tablespoons water
60g egg whites (2)
1 teaspoon instant coffee

FOR THE COFFEE CREAM

100ml semi-skimmed milk
25g ground Arabica coffee
3 teaspoons instant coffee
1 whole egg + 1 egg yolk
50g caster sugar
235g butter
25ml single cream (35% fat)

TO DECORATE

Cocoa powder
Icing sugar

PREPARE THE TIN

Butter and flour a Teflon® sandwich tin, 4cm high and 18cm in diameter.

FOR THE COFFEE SPONGE BASE

In a saucepan, melt the butter over a medium heat then heat for 1 to 2 minutes whisking constantly until it turns the colour of hazelnuts and develops a nutty flavour. Off the heat, add the instant coffee. In a mixing bowl, combine the ground hazelnuts, icing sugar and 60g of the brown sugar. Add the egg yolks and 25g of the egg whites and whisk vigorously. Pour in the browned butter while still hot in two or three batches, continuing to whisk vigorously. Incorporate the sifted flour, fleur de sel and baking powder.

WHISK THE EGG WHITES

Whisk the remaining 100g egg whites to soft peaks, incorporating at the start 15g brown sugar. Add the remaining 15g brown sugar. Fold the meringue mixture into the previous mixture in two batches: the first $1/3$ with the whisk to soften the dough, then delicately stir in the remaining $2/3$ with a spatula.

BAKE THE SPONGE

Pour this mixture into the cake tin to a depth of no more than 2cm. Bake in the oven at 170°C (gas mark 3 to 4) for about 30 minutes. When it is done, wait five minutes before carefully turning it out of the tin and removing the paper.

FOR THE HAZELNUT AND FLEUR DE SEL STREUSEL (SEE PAGE 212)

FOR THE ITALIAN MERINGUE (SEE PAGE 114)

FOR THE COFFEE INFUSION

In a saucepan, bring the semi-skimmed milk to the boil then, off the heat, add the ground coffee and the instant coffee, stir and allow to infuse uncovered for five minutes. Strain the infusion you obtain through a stocking to remove the grounds.

START THE COFFEE CREAM

Meanwhile, whisk together the egg yolk, the whole egg and the sugar until the mixture starts to become thick and pale. Take 60ml of the coffee infusion and simmer it. Off the heat, pour the infusion over the egg mixture in two or three batches, whisking constantly. Return to the saucepan and, over a low to medium heat, stir with a wooden spatula in a figure of eight without stopping. You will feel the cream forming under your spatula (don't be afraid to take it off the heat, stirring constantly, if it thickens up too fast). Bring it to just below boiling point without at any point letting it boil. When the cream is ready, strain it into the bowl of your freestanding mixer. Cool it down by giving it a whisk in the mixer on second speed. When the cream is all but cold, about 25°C to 30°C, gradually incorporate the chunks of butter at room temperature then whisk the mixture to give it a bit more volume. Whisk up the single cream to chantilly then use a spatula to delicately stir in the coffee cream, stirring from top to bottom. Finally, incorporate the Italian meringue in the same way.

TO ASSEMBLE

Lay a (clean) cake ring on a sheet of baking parchment placed on a baking tray or very flat plate. Put the sponge base in the bottom, trimming it so that it is no more than 1.5cm thick, then pour over the coffee cream up to the top of the ring. Use a stainless steel palette knife to smooth the cream, pressing the knife over the rim of the ring. Put your cake in the fridge for 30 minutes for the cream to firm up, then scatter pieces of the streusel over the top of the cake, packing little heaps tightly together and levelling them up to the edge of the ring. Turn out the cake by heating the ring lightly with a blowtorch and, finally, sprinkle the streusel with cocoa powder then with icing sugar. Bring the cake out 20 minutes before serving.

Raspberry and Matcha Tea Cake

For 6 to 7 people
Preparation time: 25mins
Cooking time: 35mins

FOR THE DOUGH
170g slightly salted butter,
   creamed (+ for the tin)
65g brown sugar
60g icing sugar
60g ground almonds
2 eggs
1 egg yolk
15ml semi-skimmed milk
60ml single cream
110g type 45 flour (+ for the tin)
1 teaspoon baking powder
150g fresh raspberries
15g grated coconut
10-15g Matcha tea

FOR THE WHISKED EGG
   WHITES
2 egg whites
15g brown sugar

LINE THE TIN
All the ingredients must be at room temperature.
Line a 20cm long loaf tin, butter and flour it.

COMBINE THE INGREDIENTS
In a mixing bowl, whisk together the creamed butter, sugars and ground almonds until pale. Add the whole eggs and the yolk then whisk again. Incorporate the milk and single cream then add the sifted flour and baking powder, half at a time. Whisk everything for about 15 seconds.

WHISK UP THE EGG WHITES
Whisk the egg whites with the brown sugar until frothy.
Meanwhile, incorporate 90% of the raspberries into the dough then delicately add in the frothy egg whites half at a time. Three quarters fill the loaf tin, place the remaining raspberries on top and sprinkle with grated coconut.

TO BAKE
Bake in the oven at 170°C (gas mark 3 to 4) for 30 to 35 minutes, according to your oven. Wait 5 minutes before turning the cake carefully out of the mould (it will still be fragile) and allow to cool. When it is cool, use a serrated knife to cut it into 2cm thick slices and sprinkle both sides of the slices with a little Matcha tea.
Serve immediately.

Lemon Cream Choux Buns

For 6 to 7 people
Preparation time: 50mins
Refrigeration time: 2hours
Cooking time: 40mins

FOR THE CHOUX PASTRY

125ml semi-skimmed milk

125ml water

110g butter

140g flour

1 level teaspoon table salt

1 heaped teaspoon caster sugar

5 eggs

FOR THE LEMON CREAM

75g butter

120g sugar

3 small eggs

90ml lemon juice

Zest of 1 lemon

1 gelatin sheet (2g)

FOR THE COCOA CARAMEL

10g pâte de cacao

175g caster sugar

50g glucose

125ml water

A few drops red food colouring (optional)

1 knob butter

FOR THE CHOUX PASTRY

Pour the milk and water into a saucepan then the butter cut into chunks.

Bring to the boil then tip in the dry sifted ingredients (flour, salt and sugar) in one go. Mix carefully: a dough will form immediately. Continue stirring over a medium heat for 1 minute to eliminate as much moisture from the dough as possible. Now tip the dough into the bowl of the electric mixer and knead with the paddle attachment (the flat beater), incorporating the whole eggs one at a time. You should obtain an elastic, glossy choux pastry.

To check whether the pastry is ready, drag your finger quite deeply across the surface for a few centimetres: the groove you make should gently close up afterwards.

BAKE THE CHOUX BUNS

Use a piping bag to pipe choux buns 4 or 5cm in diameter on to a sheet of baking parchment placed on the baking tray. Bake in the oven for 25 minutes at 170°C (gas mark 3 to 4) and allow to cool at room temperature.

FOR THE LEMON CREAM

Melt the butter in a saucepan then, when the butter is melted, add the sugar, eggs and the lemon juice and zest.

Stirring constantly, bring the mixture to just below boiling point. At the first bubble, take it off the heat and whisk again, adding in the soaked and squeezed gelatin sheet.

Clear away and set aside until the pan is barely warm, then place cling film directly over the surface of the cream and chill for at least 2 hours.

FOR THE COCOA CARAMEL

Gently melt the pâte de cacao in a bain-marie. Meanwhile, in a saucepan, bring to the boil the caster sugar, glucose and water. Pour a little of the syrup into the melted pâte de cacao, whisk, then pour it back into the pan with the remaining syrup, stirring well to avoid lumps forming. Cook the chocolate sugar on a high heat to 110°C then reduce to a low heat and continue cooking to 130°C. Off the heat, add the food colouring and knob of butter.

TO ASSEMBLE THE CHOUX BUNS

Using a piping bag, fill the choux buns with the lemon cream from underneath. Prong each bun on the end of a skewer, dip it in the caramel then place on baking parchment. Trickle over the sugar and when it hardens, cut the trail of sugar to leave a short point. Crunchy when served.

Rich Coffee Log

For 6 or 7 people
Preparation time: 1hour 30mins
Refrigeration time: 1hour
Cooking time: 15mins

FOR THE ALMOND SPONGE
4 egg yolks
2 whole eggs
155g brown sugar
60g ground almonds
60g type 55 flour
4 egg whites
200g caramelised ground nuts
(see page 215)

FOR THE COFFEE SYRUP
100ml water
50g brown sugar
2 teaspoons instant coffee
2 tablespoons coffee liqueur
(optional)

FOR THE ITALIAN MERINGUE
100g caster sugar
3 tablespoons water
2 egg whites (60g)
1 teaspoon instant coffee

FOR THE COFFEE CREAM
100ml semi-skimmed milk
25g ground Arabica coffee
1 egg yolk
1 whole egg
50g caster sugar
3 heaped teaspoons instant
coffee
235g butter
25ml single cream (35 % fat)

FOR THE ALMOND SPONGE
Preheat the oven to 170°C (gas mark 3 to 4). In a small freestanding mixer, whisk the yolks, whole eggs and the 125g of the brown sugar to a pale emulsion then gently add the ground almonds followed by the flour. Whisk up the egg whites with the rest of the brown sugar. When they are softly peaking but above all not too stiff, delicately fold them into the sponge batter half at a time. Spread the sponge to 0.5cm thick on a sheet of baking parchment placed on your oven baking tray. Bake for 8 to 10 minutes, according to your oven. Allow to cool then turn it over on to another sheet of baking paper and delicately remove the paper used for baking. Set aside.

FOR THE COFFEE SYRUP
Bring the water and brown sugar to the boil in a saucepan. Off the heat, add the instant coffee and the coffee liqueur. Set aside and allow to cool then strain the syrup you obtain through a fine-mesh sieve.

FOR THE ITALIAN MERINGUE (SEE PAGE 114)

FOR THE COFFEE CREAM
In a saucepan, bring the semi-skimmed milk to the boil then, off the heat, add the ground coffee, mix and allow to infuse uncovered for five minutes. Strain the infusion you obtain through a stocking to remove the grounds.

FOR THE COFFEE CREAM
Meanwhile, whisk together the egg yolk, whole egg and sugar until the mixture starts to become thick and pale. Take off 60ml of the coffee infusion and heat again until it simmers. Off the heat, pour the infusion over the previous mixture in two or three batches, whisking vigorously the whole time. Return to the saucepan and, over a low to medium heat, stir with a wooden spatula in a figure of eight without stopping. You will feel the cream forming under your spatula (don't be afraid to take it off the heat, stirring constantly, if it thickens up too fast). Bring it to just below boiling point without at any stage letting it boil. When the cream is ready, strain it into the bowl of your freestanding mixer. Cool it down (40 °C is the right temperature) by giving it a gentle whisk on the first speed. When the cream is just lukewarm, add the instant coffee then gradually incorporate the chunks of butter at room temperature. Whisk the mixture to give it a bit more volume. Whisk up the single cream to chantilly then use a spatula to delicately stir in the coffee cream, stirring from top to bottom. Finally, fold in the Italian meringue in the same way.

ROLL UP THE LOG
Lay out your sponge in front of you on a sheet of baking parchment on a totally flat surface. Brush the sponge all over with coffee syrup without drowning it. Using a stainless steel spatula, spread the coffee cream over the whole surface to within 1cm of all four sides. Roll the sponge up tightly like a Swiss roll (use the baking parchment to help you). Coat the roll in a thin layer of cream, wrap it in cling film and put it in the fridge for at least an hour. When the log is quite cold, trim both ends with a hot knife. Finally, roll it in the caramelised ground nuts to coat all over and put it back in the fridge until 15 minutes before serving.

CONFECTIONERY

Praline Paste

For about 1kg
Preparation time: 25mins
Cooking time: 30mins
Cooling time: 1hour

400g caster sugar
100ml water
300g whole raw hazelnuts
300g whole raw almonds

FOR THE SYRUP
In a copper pot (which has the advantage of being a perfect heat conductor) or failing that, a cast-iron pan, bring the sugar and water to the boil. Use a kitchen thermometer to take the temperature. When it reaches 116°C, add the whole hazelnuts and almonds.

COOK THE NUTS
Carefully coat the nuts in the sugar syrup then cook everything for 20 minutes, stirring constantly with a wooden spoon to prevent the almonds and hazelnuts from burning.

TO CARAMELISE
The sugar will pale a few minutes after you have added the nuts and finally caramelise throughout. After cooking, the nuts will be glossy and a lovely rich caramel colour.

PROCESS THE MIXTURE OBTAINED
Tip the caramelised almonds and hazelnuts on to a Teflon® baking tray then spread them out evenly to speed up the cooling process. Allow about an hour. When they are quite cold, pulse the nuts in a blender in three stages so the paste doesn't get too hot, to obtain a rich creamy praline paste.

Rhubarb Paste

For about 500g
Preparation time: 30mins
Cooking time: 50mins

500g fresh (or frozen) rhubarb
40ml water (if using frozen
    rhubarb, 60ml water)
Juice of ½ (small) lemon
160g caster sugar
1 pinch fleur de sel
2.5 sheets gelatin (5g)

FOR THE RHUBARB
Peel the rhubarb then cut it into 5cm chunks. Cut each chunk lengthwise in two.

COOK THE RHUBARB
Put the rhubarb into a saucepan over a medium heat, add water, lemon juice, sugar and fleur de sel and simmer for 50 minutes. Stir evenly with a spatula until almost all the cooking juice has evaporated. The aim is to obtain a thick paste with a soft texture but firm enough to hold its shape, as if you were making a quenelle, for instance.

INCORPORATE THE GELATIN
Soften the sheets of gelatin in a bowl of cold water. Wring them out by hand and stir them into the compote. Stir thoroughly and pour the mixture into a mixing bowl. Cover with cling film and refrigerate until needed.

Caramels with Salted Butter

For about 600g caramels
Preparation time: 15mins
Cooling time: 12hours

1 vanilla pod
275ml single cream, 35% fat
200g caster sugar
100g glucose syrup
1 pinch fleur de sel
45g slightly salted butter
450g crushed macadamia nuts

BOIL THE INGREDIENTS
Split the vanilla pod in two, scrape out the halves and reserve the seeds. In a saucepan, bring the cream, caster sugar and vanilla seeds to the boil then add the glucose, the fleur de sel then the butter. Continue cooking to 114°C, stirring constantly. Add the macadamia nuts.

ALLOW THE CARAMEL TO COOL
Immediately, pour the caramel you obtain on to a sheet of baking parchment in a frame or mould to a depth of 10mm. Set aside in a reasonably cool place but as dry as possible for about 12 hours for a crust to form.

CUT THE CARAMEL
Use a knife to cut strips 13cm long by 1cm wide. Store your caramels in a dry place.

Vanilla Crème Pâtissière

For 600g cream
Preparation time: 15mins
Cooking time: 10mins
Infusion time: 15mins
Refrigeration time: 1hour

500ml semi-skimmed milk
½ vanilla pod
4 egg yolks
40g caster sugar
45g flour

HEAT THE MILK
Pour the milk into a saucepan with the split and scraped vanilla pod. Bring to the boil then take it straight off the heat. Allow to infuse off the heat for 15 minutes.

COMBINE THE REMAINING INGREDIENTS
In a mixing bowl, whisk together the egg yolks and sugar until pale. Add the flour and stir well to a homogenous paste then add half the still-hot milk with the half vanilla pod removed. Mix again then pour everything into the pan of milk.

HEAT THE CUSTARD
Bring the custard to the boil for 2 minutes, whisking constantly. When it is quite thick, pour it into a gratin dish for it to spread out and cool more quickly. Cover with cling film, patting it down on to the surface of the custard, then refrigerate for about an hour.

Hazelnut and Fleur de Sel Streusel

For about 200g
Preparation time: 15mins

50g flour
50g brown sugar
2 pinches fleur de sel
65g ground hazelnuts
50g slightly salted butter at
    room temperature

COMBINE THE DRY INGREDIENTS
In a mixing bowl, combine the flour, sugar, salt and ground hazelnuts.

INCORPORATE THE SOFTENED BUTTER
Now, add the butter cut into chunks (which should be very soft) and knead everything with your hands until the butter adheres to the dry ingredients without forming a dough; it should be the consistency of a crumble topping.

Sweet Chocolate Ice Cream

For about 1litre
Preparation time: 20mins
Cooking time: 15mins
Freezing time: 12hours

550ml semi-skimmed milk
250ml single cream, 35% fat
1 vanilla pod
½ level teaspoon fleur de sel
8 egg yolks
80g caster sugar
80g milk chocolate, chopped
220g dark chocolate, chopped

FOR THE CRÈME ANGLAISE

In a saucepan, bring the milk and cream to the boil with the split and scraped vanilla pod and the fleur de sel. Meanwhile, whisk the egg yolks with the sugar until thick and pale. When the milk and cream mixture reaches boiling point, pour it over the pale egg yolks a half or third at a time, continuing to whisk vigorously.

Return the mixture to the pan over a low to medium heat and stir with a wooden spatula in a figure of eight until the cream coats the spatula. While cooking the crème anglaise, stir it constantly to prevent the yolks from coagulating. Gradually, the mixture will thicken and the surface froth disappear. You will feel the cream forming under your spatula, but take it off the heat, continuing to stir, if it thickens up too quickly. This ice cream gets its thick, silky consistency from the cooking process. You should bring it to just below boiling point without at any point letting it boil.

INCORPORATE THE CHOCOLATE

When the cream is cooked, strain it over the chopped milk and dark chocolate then whisk for 30 seconds to create an emulsion. Allow to cool at room temperature, stirring from time to time.

PLACE IN THE FREEZER

When the mixture is cold, cover with cling film and allow to thicken and mature in the freezer for 12 hours. Twenty to 25 minutes before serving, churn the ice cream.

Nougat

For 1kg nougat
Preparation time: 1hour
Cooking time: 25mins

180g whole raw almonds
50g whole pistachios
80g whole hazelnuts
250g caster sugar
120g glucose (or caster sugar)
85ml water
210g acacia honey
75g egg whites
Icing sugar

TOAST THE NUTS
Hull the nuts and dry-toast them for 2 minutes in a non-stick frying pan.

HEAT THE SUGARS
In a saucepan, heat the caster sugar with the glucose and water until it reaches 144°C on a sugar thermometer. Meanwhile, heat the honey in a saucepan until it reaches 122°C.

FOR THE MERINGUE
Tip the egg whites into a Pyrex® mixing bowl. Using an electric whisk, whisk them to peaks on medium speed. When they are softly peaking but not too stiff, pour in the cooked sugar in a single stream (when the bubbles of syrup have disappeared), whisking on medium speed. When the honey, still on the heat, reaches 122°C and the bubbles have disappeared, pour it over the whisked egg whites in the same way.

WHISK THE MERINGUE UNTIL STIFF
Put the meringue in a mixing bowl in a bain-marie and whisk at low speed until stiff. You want to end up with a fairly firm paste (the meringue should form a slightly pliable ball that doesn't stick to your fingers). This process will take about 30 to 40 minutes in all. Caution: don't continue this stage for too long, because you need to be able to work the nougat paste and cut it up.

INCORPORATE THE NUTS
Now add the whole nuts. Stir briskly and pour the nutty nougat paste on to the work surface covered with a sheet of baking parchment. Coat your hands with icing sugar then roll a fat sausage between the palms of your hand.

TO FINISH
Place the nougat sausage inside a frame or mould lined with baking parchment, place another sheet of baking parchment on top and roll it out with the rolling pin. Allow the nougat to rest at room temperature in a dry place.

CUT THE NOUGAT
Turn the nougat out of the frame or mould, using baking parchment to help you remove it, and cut the nougat into pieces with a large knife.

Red Fruit Compote

For about 350g
Preparation time: 20mins
Maceration time: 1 night
Cooking time: 15mins

175g strawberries

50g raspberries

2 bunches redcurrants

15g blackcurrant seeds

120g granulated sugar

1 teaspoon lime juice

2 teaspoons lemon juice

½ teaspoon lemon zest

½ teaspoon pectin (Vitpris®) (4g)

MACERATE THE SOFT FRUIT

The day before: in a mixing bowl, carefully combine the soft fruit and half the sugar, the lime juice and lemon juice and the zests. Cover the bowl with cling film then refrigerate overnight.

TO COOK

The same day: in a saucepan set over a medium heat, cook the macerated fruit in their macerating juice for about 10 minutes. Mix the pectin with the remaining sugar and add it to the fruit. Bring to the boil then take the pan off the heat.

Pour the mixture into a mixing bowl then cover with cling film, patting it down directly on to the surface before putting the compote in the fridge.

Marbled Praline Ice Cream

For about 1litre
Preparation time: 30mins
Cooking time: 20mins
Freezing time: 12hours

500ml semi-skimmed milk
250ml single cream
3 vanilla pods
10 egg yolks
120g caster sugar
200g praline paste
(see page 172)

HEAT THE VANILLA CREAM

In a saucepan, bring the milk and single cream to the boil with the split and scraped vanilla pods. Meanwhile, whisk the egg yolks with the sugar until thick and pale.

When the milk and cream mixture boils, take it off the heat and pour it over the egg yolk mixture a half or third at a time, whisking constantly.

THICKEN THE CREAM

Return the cream to the pan over a low to medium heat and stir with a wooden spatula in a figure of eight without stopping so that the yolks don't coagulate. The mixture will gradually thicken up and the froth disappear. You will feel the cream forming under your spatula, but take it off the heat, continuing to stir, if it thickens up too quickly. The true secret to the thick, silky consistency of this ice cream is in the cooking. You should bring it to just below boiling without at any point letting it boil.

CHILL THE CREAM

When the cream is cooked, strain it then whisk for 30 seconds and allow to cool at room temperature (giving it the occasional stir).

When the mixture is cold, cover it with cling film and allow to thicken up and mature in the freezer for 12 hours.

CHURN THE ICE CREAM

Thirty minutes before serving, churn the ice cream. Just before taking it out, pour the praline paste over it, churn for a few seconds but don't let the praline blend completely so that the ice cream retains a marbled effect.

Clear away and store in the freezer.

Citrus Fruit Jellies

Makes 225 squares
Preparation time: 25mins

205ml water

140ml orange juice

65ml grapefruit juice

25ml lemon juice

10ml lime juice

½ vanilla pod

Zest of 1 orange

9g pectin

420g caster sugar

100g glucose

FOR THE TARTARIC
  ACID SOLUTION

2g tartaric acid

2g water

TO COAT

500g caster sugar

10g tartaric acid

BOIL THE FRUIT JUICE

In a saucepan, boil the water, fruit juices, seeds of the half vanilla pod and the orange zest then sprinkle in the pectin combined with 45g of the caster sugar. Whisk well to prevent lumps forming.

ADD THE SUGAR

Add the remaining caster sugar in two or three batches then stir in the glucose. Heat the mixture to 110°C, whisking vigorously the whole time so that it doesn't stick and burn.

ADD THE TARTARIC ACID

Incorporate the tartaric acid solution (the acid is a catalyst for pectin). Whisk vigorously for a few seconds then pour the fruit paste on to a sheet of baking parchment between 4 strips to guide you (a square of about 30 x 30cm to 1cm thick).

CUT AND COAT THE FRUIT JELLIES

Allow to cool and cut into squares with 2cm sides. Coat the fruit jelly squares with a mixture of caster sugar and tartaric acid.

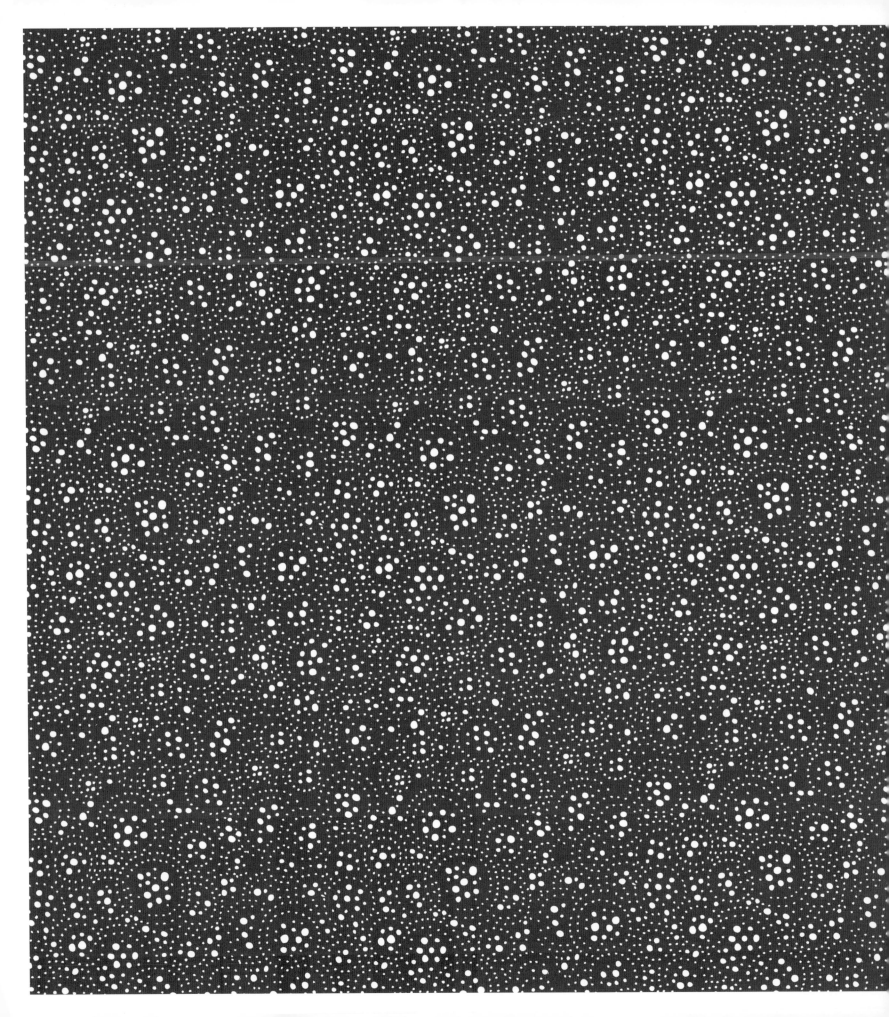

LESSONS ON TASTE

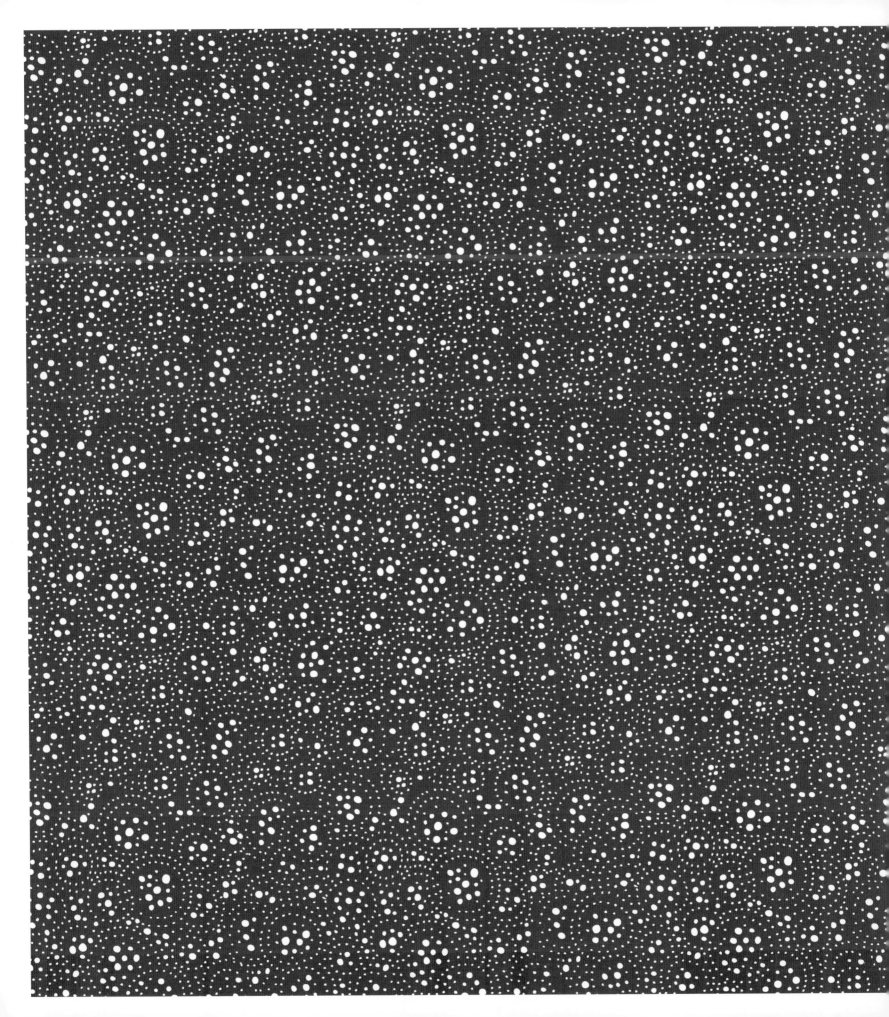

PRODUCTS

NOIX DE COCO RÂPÉE CARAMÉLISÉE

AMANDES NATURES

CRISTAUX D'AMANDES CAR

LA PÂTISSERIE DES RÊVES

PAR PHILIPPE CONTICINI

LA PÂTISSERIE DES RÊVES

PAR PHILIPPE CONTICINI

SUCRE ROUX

LA PÂTISSERIE DES RÊVES

PAR PHILIPPE CONTICINI

AMANDES ENTIÈRES CARA

LA PÂTISSERIE DES RÊVES

PAR PHILIPPE CONTICINI

CRISTAUX DE NOISETTES CARAM

LA PÂTISSERIE DES RÊVES

PAR PHILIPPE CONTICINI

SUCRE PERLÉ

LA PÂTISSERIE DES RÊVES

PAR PHILIPPE CONTICINI

NOISETTES NA

LA PÂTISSERIE DES

CRISTAUX DE PISTAC

LA PÂTISSE

SUCRE PÉTILLANT

LA PÂTISSERIE DES RÊVES

PAR PHILIPPE CONTICINI

NOISETTES ENTIÈRES CARAM

Chocolate

Chocolate is an extraordinary product with no equivalent in cooking or baking. For me, it's a major ingredient. You can play with its more or less pronounced bitterness and singular flavour and use it as a spice or a condiment or, on the contrary, give it pride of place. You can experiment with the texture and make it runny in some recipes and crunchy in others. It really is a fascinating product and a constant source of discovery for me.

TAMING ITS BITTERNESS

I actually came to the bitter taste of dark chocolate quite late. Even now when I try a bar of dark chocolate, I don't go beyond 68%. I like my chocolate to be fruity, not too sharp but full of character. I like it to be melting, smooth on the palate and silky with a good cocoa-butter content. When I try a chocolate, I don't bite into it, I let it melt between my tongue and palate to experience all the stages of fabrication.

CHOCOLATE AS A CONDIMENT

When I work, I like to go to the limits of what it has to offer. At La Pâtisserie des Rêves, I give it a starring role, notably in my 'grand cru' recipe, an intensely chocolaty cake.

What interests me most, however, is to use it as a condiment, a bit the way a painter might use a primary colour. When I'm working on a new confection, I generally choose a very fruity chocolate that's not too bitter for a dense, rich sponge with a crispy chocolate-based topping of praline and fleur de sel, for the richness and seasoning from which to construct a flavour that is uniquely mine, one I like and that brings me pleasure.

Although I cook it or use it in ganaches, I also like it raw to emphasise its texture and add it grated or crushed to a mousse or sponge.

AT HOME: USE A CHOCOLATE YOU LIKE

So, while in confectionery its quality, flavour and origin are clearly crucial, in baking, especially at home, you don't have to invest in 'grands crus' chocolate. The best chocolate for your cakes will really be the one you like. If you like your chocolate bitter, use one with a high cocoa content, but take it from me: there's no rule against preferring a sweeter, milder chocolate. You can even use a combination of dark and milk chocolate.

Wheat Flour

In pâtisserie, flour is used as an ingredient to structure creams, sponges and cakes. But it is specifically associated with dough-making. In that context, the aim is to utilise the strength it provides according to the gluten content. Depending on the result you're aiming for, you will use different flours. So, traditionally, strong flour (type 45) is associated with leavened bread (croissant, brioche and kugelhof dough or puff pastry), whereas type 55 flours (the higher the figure, the lower the gluten content) are more suitable for sponge mixtures, loaf cakes, choux pastry or biscuits.

A ROASTED FLAVOUR

But apart from being a basic ingredient, wheat that is roasted during cooking gives a preparation a unique and significant flavour. On that basis, I therefore like using whole-wheat flours for their richer flavour, especially for making biscuits. And when I make pastry cases, I take special care with the cooking. I like the flour to be well roasted but not over-cooked, because that upsets the balance of flavours and makes the pastry bitter.

OTHER TYPES OF FLOUR

Depending on what you need it for, you can also use other types of flour or starch, each of which has its own characteristics. Rice flour, for example, has a crunchier texture. It absorbs moisture better and is ideal for doughnut batter. Cornflour is light and a good thickener. I certainly suggest it for preparing creams, although it doesn't stand up to prolonged cooking. For myself, I recommend using it with wheat flour (half and half), to lighten the mixture but preserve the texture. Potato flour is even lighter than cornflour. Also a good thickener, it can be perfectly suitable for biscuit dough or pancake batter.

Fleur de Sel

Fleur de sel is the name given to crystals collected by hand from the saltpan then drained and dried in the sun. Famed for its delicate flavour with a hint of violets, it has a lower sodium content than table salt or coarse salt.

TEXTURE AND LONG FINISH

Since I started working with this product, I've stopped using coarse salt and hardly ever use table salt.

In my recipes, I appreciate it as a flavour enhancer with a long finish. But I use it above all for its structure and crisp texture. So, as far as possible, I avoid melting it.

Brown Sugars

There are a number of brown sugars. Produced from sugar cane or sugar beet, they may or may not be refined. They include cassonade (similar to Demerara), which is granulated sugar made up of 95% sucrose and 5% mineral salts with plant residue (fibres, etc) that give it its colour, moist appearance and its flavour of rum and vanilla. It is lightly flavoured and not very dark, but it is very dry so caramelises well. Cassonade is the ideal sugar to use in crème brûlée.

VERGEOISE

Produced from cooked beet syrup, vergeoise is favoured by chefs in northern France and Belgium where it is used in Speculoos, pancakes, waffles and crème brûlée. It has a soft texture and its colour depends on how much it is cooked. It has a rich caramel flavour (more pronounced when it is brown – it is also available as 'vergeoise blonde' or light vergeoise) and a rather moist appearance. It gives biscuits their crumbly texture.

MUSCOVADO

Obtained by the total evaporation of the water content in sugarcane juice, this is an unrefined sugar and rich in vitamins and minerals. It is brown in colour and tastes of vanilla, old rum and liquorice. Light muscovado has a very caramelised, slightly bitter flavour, which is why I never use it. To my mind, it is not as tasty.

MOLASSES

This is a thick syrup and a residue from refining the cane. In my entire career, I have only ever used it in a single dessert. I made a jelly as a condiment for a dessert based on walnuts, caramel, figs and Armagnac.

BROWN SUGAR WITH FLAVOUR

At home, I recommend using Alter Eco® brown sugar which is particularly aromatic and flavourful. I love its fine, dry sandy texture, ideal for crunchy, sweet short-crust pastry.

Caramel

Produced from sugar, caramel is a key ingredient in baking. Personally, I use it mostly for the taste, although of course it gives a preparation its structure.

HOW MUCH COOKING?

My favourite caramel is sugar cooked with water to 175°C (off the heat, it goes up to 176°C), at which point it turns a dark copper colour and loses some of its sweetening capacity but is not yet bitter.
I then marry it with fleur de sel, passion fruit, citrus fruit, chocolate or nuts.

MY SOFT CARAMEL

For soft caramel, I melt the caramel dry. My aim is to heat it until it holds together firmly. I add milk, cream and butter to cool it then I re-heat it to the required temperature to obtain the consistency I want.

Citrus Fruit

This family of fruit has become essential to me. Over time, I have discovered the importance of citrus for baking and more generally, for cooking. With age, I have learnt to appreciate, understand and master the bitterness, tanginess and the astringency and aromatic power of these unique fruits.

A WIDE VARIETY

The citrus universe is vast. It offers a wide range of taste and flavours from which to construct luscious bitterness. I talk about it in general terms rather than taking each fruit individually: I put citrus fruit into the equation to obtain a tasty result that most people will enjoy.

MY GOURMET EQUATION

Power of the fruit + bitterness + tanginess = powerful flavour, long finish, heightened senses and aromas.

Nuts

Galettes, pithiviers, financiers, sablés… pastry chefs use nuts in their recipes in a plethora of ways. For myself, I use them daily in sweet short-crust pastry (pâte brisée and pâte sablée), or in financiers with pistachios, hazelnuts and almonds.

MY ALMOND AND HAZELNUT PRALINE

But first and foremost, I use them to make praline (based on 50-50 quantities of almonds and hazelnuts), which I use as a condiment in certain preparations and especially in chocolate. You're not necessarily aware of it, but you'd miss it if it wasn't there. I also use almonds on their own to make almond butter which I like for its silky consistency, and almond cream which absorbs the fruit juice in a fruit tart, for example.

WALNUTS

Apart from almonds or hazelnuts which I use a lot, I also work with walnuts, in sponge mixtures rather than for pralines. I crush them, but quite coarsely to preserve and emphasise the texture of the nuts in a sponge mixture.

PINE NUTS

As for pine nuts, I like them lightly toasted in the oven (at 150°C–160°C, gas mark 2-3) for 12 to 15 minutes to toast them right through.

Butter

THE TWO VIRTUES OF BUTTER

Again, butter is essential in baking. For me, it has two virtues: it stabilizes the flavours and it makes a pâtisserie soft and moist. On that basis, butter is vital to the sensation in the mouth, making a pâtisserie more or less melting or more or less grainy.

PRIORITISING FLAVOUR

So, I use butter in several ways. When I make a biscuit or a croissant, the first thing I want is to bring out the flavour of the butter, which is crucial to both. So, I choose a high quality product, like Échiré or Isigny butter.

CONSISTENCY

When I'm making a sponge base, Tarte Tatin or fruit tagine, on the other hand, butter then becomes an important ingredient for the structure or for the overall flavour, but not for its own flavour. So, I choose a more classic butter, good quality of course, but not necessarily 'grand cru'.

CREAM AND CARAMEL

To make a caramel, I advise using a top quality, slightly salted butter, and the same goes for making creams. In crème pâtissière, for instance, I always incorporate chilled butter at the end of the process to form an emulsion and make the cream silkier.

MY PREFERENCE FOR SLIGHTLY-SALTED BUTTER

I should add that over the years, my tastes have changed. These days, I opt increasingly for slightly-salted butter, whereas I used not to. I just prefer it now. And when I use unsalted butter, I always add fleur de sel, both as a flavour enhancer and for its long finish (see the Fleur de Sel section above).

BUTTER REPLACEMENTS

On rare occasions and only to obtain a crisper, crunchier texture, I have been known to replace butter with margarine. Because margarine melts at a higher temperature, it makes for a drier puff pastry. But it has a less interesting flavour. So, you should keep that kind of pastry for specific preparations with lots of flavour.

Vanilla

Whether it has a starring or a secondary role (essential) in a recipe, vanilla obviously comes into its own in baking.

FOR A MILDER FLAVOUR
Apart from its unique flavour, I often use vanilla to take the edge off full-bodied (tangy) flavours in a cake. That way, I can use less sugar.

FOR GENERAL SEASONING
I also use it as a general seasoning ingredient. Don't forget that vanilla is a spice. So, you don't necessarily notice it, but it is very important.

ONLY THE BEST
And, of course, I use it for its flavour in cakes and pastries where it has pride of place. I used to use Bourbon vanilla a lot, but these days, I prefer Tahiti, which I consider more highly flavoured. When I buy it (not that you always have the choice in shops for the general public), you should choose pods that are pliable, glossy and fat though not too fat because you want them to have a concentrated flavour.

Spices

Spices occupy a very important place in my baking. To list a few, I use cumin, cinnamon, caraway, vanilla (see above) cloves, nutmeg (grated or mace), ginger, coriander seeds and liquorice. I'm also a fan of mixed spice blends like pain d'épices, quatre-épices (four-spice blend: allspice, cloves, nutmeg and ginger) and cinq-épices (five-spice blend, including star anise, cinnamon, fennel and cloves).

PRIORITISING THEIR UNIQUE FLAVOURS
Usually, I think of gastronomy, and more generally baking, the way a painter produces a painting. The ingredients are the primary colours which I mix to produce innovative hues (flavours). Above all, however, I use spices (apart from vanilla and liquorice, which I also use to sweeten a preparation) for their unique flavours. I want people to notice them, and I give them an important place.

TOBACCO AS A SPICE
For a special dessert, I have been known to use tobacco (I used Amsterdamer) infusing it cold for 9 seconds, to obtain a piquant flavour not unlike ginger.

MY FAVOURITE FLAVOUR COMBINATIONS
Rhubarb + clove + mango + ginger
Peach + liquorice
Coconut + ginger
Chocolate + ginger
Pear + pain d'épices

Candied carrots + coriander seed
Caraway + soft fruit
Caraway + citrus fruit
Cumin + pink pomelo

Alcohol

I use alcohol sparingly. Personally, I don't like spirits, but I'm very interested in their flavours for baking purposes.

WHAT ALCOHOL DO I USE?

There's Kirsch, Cointreau, Sherry and some brandies. I also like whisky and some aperitifs, like Guignolet, Ricard and Martini. But my three essentials are rum which I use in a jus with fleur de sel, fruit liqueurs (blackcurrant, blackberry and peach) to accompany fruit desserts, and Grand Marnier to flavour pancake batter, for example.

MY PET COMBINATIONS

Buckwheat + apples + whisky + hops

Orange + vanilla + rum + fleur de sel

Turkish delight + dark beer

Pomelo + coconut + cashew + whisky + vanilla

Chestnut paste with black sesame + candied cherries + ginger + Martini

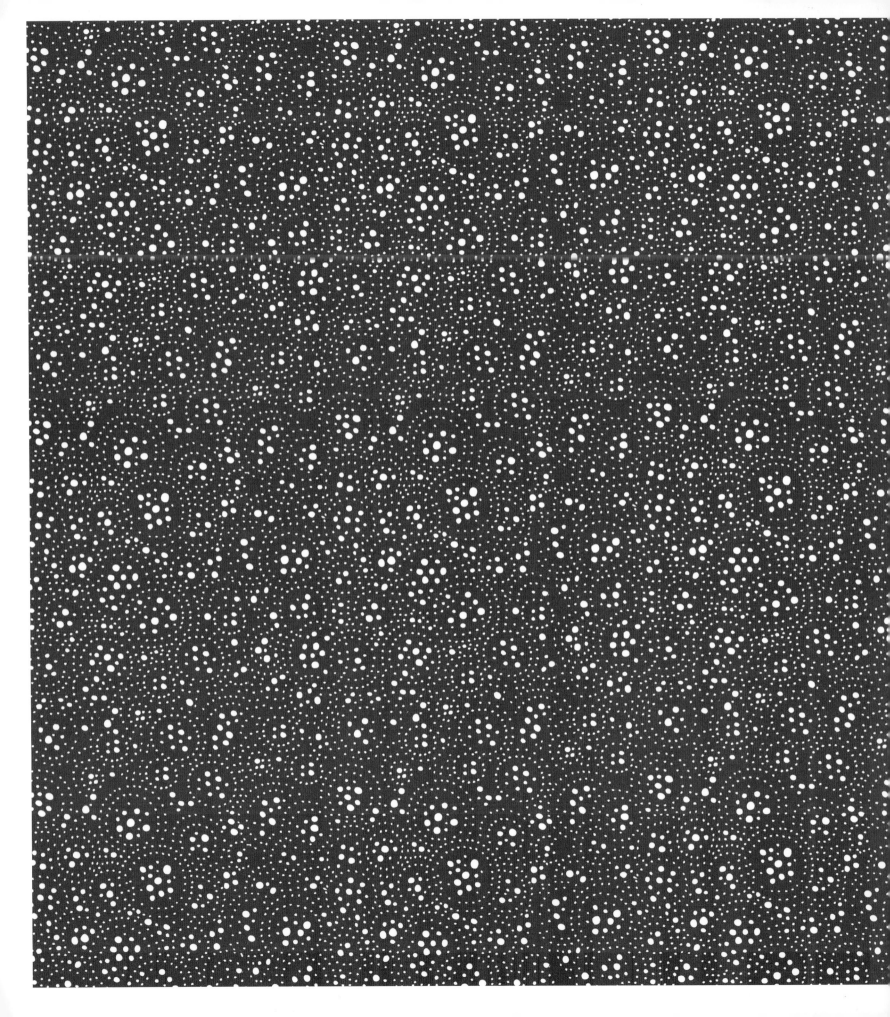

BASIC RECIPES
STEP BY STEP

PÂTE SUCRÉE

For 500g pastry – Preparation: 15mins – Refrigeration time: 3hours

1 vanilla pod • 140g softened butter • 90g icing sugar • 40g ground almonds • 1 large egg • 1 egg yolk • 4 pinches fleur de sel • 230g flour

1 SCRAPE OUT THE VANILLA SEEDS
Place 1 vanilla pod on the work surface, crush it with the flat of a knife blade, open the pod and scrape out and reserve the seeds.

2 COMBINE THE INGREDIENTS
In a mixing bowl, cream 140g softened butter with a whisk. Stir in the vanilla seeds and 90g icing sugar (1). Add 40g ground almonds, 1 large egg and 1 egg yolk, whisk again then add 4 pinches fleur de sel and 230g flour half at a time.

3 COMBINE THOROUGHLY
Continue whisking until the mixture is homogenous but not totally smooth (2).

4 'FRAISAGE' OF THE PASTRY
Lay the pastry on the floured work surface (3) and flatten it roughly with the palm of your hand, pushing down on it three or four times.

5 ALLOW THE PASTRY TO REST
Roll the pastry into a ball (4), wrap it in cling film then refrigerate for at least 3 hours before use.

INVERSE PUFF PASTRY IN THE ELECTRIC MIXER

For 1.5kg pastry – Preparation time: 50mins – Refrigeration time: 5hours 30mins – Cooking time: 3hours 30mins

400g flour • 1 heaped teaspoon salt • 250ml single cream • 600g softened butter • 200g flour

FOR THE PUFF PASTRY

1 In the bowl of the electric mixer fitted with the paddle attachment (the flat beater), combine 400g flour and the spoonful of salt. Count one minute then add 1 tablespoon water and the single cream a little at a time. Take the dough out of the mixer bowl and knead it by hand on the floured work surface. You should obtain quite a firm texture. Shape the dough into a ball and wrap it in cling film. Chill for 2 hours in the fridge.

FOR THE BEURRE MANIÉ (KNEADED BUTTER)
2 (SEE PAGE 223)

ROLL OUT THE PASTRY

3 Take the dough out of the fridge and roll it out on the floured work surface (1). You should obtain a square with 25cm sides (2). Lightly flour the rolled-out pastry.

LAY THE PASTRY ON THE BEURRE MANIÉ

4 Take the butter out of the fridge and place it on the floured work surface. Lay the pastry over the butter and fold the edges of the butter in to the centre of the pastry, so that the edges meet. Roll out the pastry to obtain a long rectangle 25 x 70cm. Fold the top third into the middle of the pastry, then do the same with the bottom third (3). Give the folded pastry a quarter turn then roll it out to obtain a long rectangle 25 x 70cm again and fold it into three layers like a wallet. Give it a second turn, the same as the first. Roll out the pastry, fold it and wrap it in cling film, then refrigerate for 30 minutes.

FOR THE THIRD AND FOURTH TURNS

5 Take the pastry out of the fridge, roll it out, fold it and give it a third turn and then a fourth (4). Wrap it in cling film and refrigerate for 30 minutes. Give it a fifth and sixth turn. Allow 30 minutes in the fridge before use.

SWEET CHOUX PASTRY IN THE ELECTRIC MIXER

For about 800g choux pastry – Preparation: 15mins – Cooking: 8mins

140g flour • 1 heaped teaspoon granulated sugar • 1 level teaspoon table salt • 110g butter • 125ml milk • 125ml water • 5 eggs

1

SIFT THE DRY INGREDIENTS
Place a sieve over a mixing bowl and use it to sift 140g flour, 1 heaped teaspoon granulated sugar and 1 level teaspoon table salt. Combine.

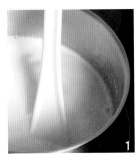

2

HEAT THE MILK, WATER AND BUTTER
Cut 110g butter into chunks. Put milk, water and the butter chunks into a saucepan. Heat on high (1).

3

TIP THE FLOUR INTO THE SAUCEPAN
When it boils, tip the contents of the mixing bowl into the pan in one go (2).

4

ELIMINATE THE MOISTURE FROM THE DOUGH
Stir carefully using a wooden spoon: a dough will form immediately (3). Continue stirring over a medium heat for 1 minute until the dough comes away from the sides of the pan.

5

FINISH MIXING IN THE ELECTRIC MIXER
Now tip the dough into the bowl of the electric mixer, then knead with the paddle attachment (the flat beater in the mixer), incorporating 5 whole eggs one at a time. You should obtain a pliable, glossy choux pastry (4).

VANILLA CRÈME PÂTISSIÈRE

For 600g cream – Preparation time: 15mins – Infusion time: 15mins – Cooking time: 10 mins – Refrigeration time: 1hour

500ml milk • ½ vanilla pod • 4 egg yolks • 40g caster sugar • 45g flour • 50g butter (diced and chilled)

1 HEAT THE MILK
In a saucepan, bring together the milk and ½ vanilla pod with the seeds scraped out. Heat on a medium heat.

2 INFUSE THE VANILLA
When the milk boils, take it off the heat and allow to infuse for 15 minutes.

3 COMBINE THE EGGS AND SUGAR
In a mixing bowl, whisk together the 4 egg yolks and 40g caster sugar (1) until pale. Add 45g flour and mix thoroughly to obtain a homogenous paste (2).

4 POUR IN HALF THE MILK
Take out the vanilla pod and pour half the milk into the mixing bowl (3) while still hot. Whisk again.

5 HEAT THE CREAM
Pour this mixture into the pan and bring the cream to the boil for 2 minutes, whisking vigorously the whole time. Whisk in the diced and chilled butter in three batches.

6 ALLOW THE CREAM TO COOL
Pour the cream into a gratin dish (4) for it to spread out and cool more rapidly. Cover with cling film, patting it down on to the surface, then refrigerate for about 1 hour.

HAZELNUT AND FLEUR DE SEL STREUSEL

For about 200g streusel – Preparation time: 15mins

50g flour • 50g brown sugar • 65g ground hazelnuts • 2 pinches fleur de sel • 50g slightly salted butter

1 COMBINE THE DRY INGREDIENTS
In a mixing bowl, combine 50g flour, 50g brown sugar, 65g ground hazelnuts and 2 pinches fleur de sel (1).

2 INCORPORATE THE SOFTENED BUTTER
Now, add 50g slightly salted butter in chunks. The butter should be very soft (2). To soften, take it out of the fridge 1 hour before starting the recipe.

3 COMBINE WELL
Rub in by hand until the butter adheres to the dry ingredients (3) to form a coarse, sandy consistency similar to a crumble topping.

4 Crumble the streusel, packing the lumps tightly, on to a sheet of baking parchment lining a baking tray and cook in the oven at 150°C (gas mark 2) for 25 to 30 minutes (4).

FRUIT TAGINE

For 6 people – Preparation time: 25mins – Cooking time: 35mins

FOR THE FOAMING, TANGY BUTTER
30g butter • 50g brown sugar • 35ml lemon juice • 1 vanilla pod (from Tahiti)

FOR THE FRUIT
2 Golden Delicious apples • 175g orange segments • 175g pink pomelo segments • 65g sultanas • 25g whole blanched almonds • Juice of 1 grapefruit• Juice of 2 oranges • 1 teaspoon vanilla extract • 10g candied ginger, sliced • 40g brown sugar • 1 generous pinch ground cinnamon • 1 pinch pain d'épices spice •10 fresh mint leaves

1 **FOR THE FRUIT**
Peel and core the apples, then dice them finely. Segment the citrus fruit (orange and pomelos), removing all the white pith and taking care to catch the juice in a small bowl (1).

2 **FOR THE FOAMING BUTTER**
In a saucepan, melt the butter over a medium heat until foaming, then add the sugar and the split and scraped vanilla pod. Deglaze with the lemon juice then stir the mixture carefully with a spatula until homogenous.

3 **INCORPORATE THE FRUIT AND SPICES**
Add the diced apples to the foaming butter (2) then the sultanas and whole almonds. Reduce the mixture for 3 minutes over a medium heat then add the orange and grapefruit segments. Continue cooking for another 2 minutes, then pour in half the grapefruit and orange juice, the vanilla extract, finely sliced candied ginger, the remaining sugar then the cinnamon and pain d'épices spice (3).

4 **CONTINUE COOKING**
Turn down the heat, reduce the mixture for about 20 minutes over a low heat, stirring from time to time to prevent it sticking and moistening progressively with the remaining orange and grapefruit juice. At the end of the cooking, take off the heat, and add the fresh mint leaves (4).

PÂTE À FONCER IN THE ELECTRIC MIXER

For 500g pastry
Preparation time: 15mins

200g flour
150g butter
1 tablespoon icing sugar
1 teaspoon table salt
55ml water
1 tablespoon white vinegar

1 SIFT THE FLOUR
Place a fine-mesh sieve over a mixing bowl and sift the flour.

2 MAKE THE PASTRY IN THE ELECTRIC MIXER
Fit your mixer with the paddle attachment. Put 150g butter into the bowl and knead at low speed until very creamy.

3 ADD THE DRY INGREDIENTS
Now, add the 200g flour, 1 tablespoon icing sugar and 1 teaspoon table salt. Continue kneading for 2 to 3 minutes to obtain a coarse, sandy mixture.

4 INCORPORATE THE VINEGAR WATER
Combine 55ml water and 1 tablespoon white vinegar. Pour this into the bowl of the mixer and knead at low speed for 2 minutes, but don't let the pastry fully bind together.

5 'FRAISAGE' OF THE PASTRY
Take the pastry out of the bowl and place it on the floured work surface. Flatten it roughly with the palm of your hand, pushing down on it three or four times. Wrap it in cling film and refrigerate until needed.

CARAMELISED GROUND MIXED NUTS

For about 200g ground nuts
Preparation time: 30mins
Cooking time: 50mins

FOR THE CARAMELISED GROUND NUTS

75g raw whole almonds

75g raw whole hazelnuts

95g caster sugar

25ml water

1 FOR THE CARAMELISED GROUND MIXED NUTS

Start by roasting the almonds and hazelnuts right through. Put them on baking parchment in the oven at 150°C (gas mark 2) for about 25 minutes, according to your oven, of course.
Bring the sugar and water to the boil in a saucepan and heat this syrup to 116°C using a sugar thermometer. Add the roasted almonds and hazelnuts when they are cool.

2 FOR THE CARAMELISED NUTS

Carefully coat the nuts with the sugar syrup, then heat everything for 20 minutes, stirring continually with a wooden spoon to prevent the nuts burning.
The sugar will turn pale a few minutes after you add the nuts then caramelise all over. At the end of the cooking time, the nuts will be glossy and have turned a dark copper colour.

3 PULSE THE NUTS

Tip the caramelised almonds and hazelnuts on to a Teflon tray or a sheet of baking parchment then spread them out so that they cool more rapidly. Take care not to burn yourself – they will be piping hot.
When they are quite cold, pulse the nuts to a fine powder in a processor, in two stages to stop them getting too hot.

CRÈME PRALINÉE

For about 400g cream
Preparation time: 25mins
Cooking time: 8mins
Refrigeration time: 1hour

1 sheet gelatin
155ml semi-skimmed milk
2 egg yolks
30g caster sugar
15g cornflour
80g almond-and-hazelnut praline
70g cold butter

1 SOFTEN THE GELATIN
Soak 1 sheet gelatin in a bowl of cold water to soften it.

2 HEAT THE MILK
Pour the semi-skimmed milk into a saucepan. Take the pan off the heat when it boils.

3 COMBINE THE EGG YOLKS AND SUGAR
In a mixing bowl, whisk together the 2 egg yolks and 30g caster sugar until pale. Now add the cornflour and continue whisking to obtain a homogenous paste then pour in half the milk while still hot. Whisk again then pour everything into the pan of milk.

4 HEAT THE CREAM
Bring the cream to the boil for 1 minute, whisking constantly. When the cream is quite thick, take it off the heat. Now incorporate the soaked and squeezed gelatin.

5 ADD THE PRALINE AND BUTTER
Add 80g almond and hazelnut praline and finally 70g cold butter cut into chunks.

6 BLEND THE CREAM
Now blend the cream with a hand-held mixer until smooth and homogenous. Pour the cream into a large dish for it to spread out and cool more quickly. Cover with cling film patting it down directly on to the surface (to stop it drying out), and refrigerate for about 1 hour.

7 WHISK BEFORE USE
When the cream is cold, whisk it in an electric mixer at medium speed for 3 minutes before use.

CRÈME ANGLAISE

For about 1litre
Preparation time: 15mins
Cooking time: 25mins

1 vanilla pod
550ml semi-skimmed milk
250ml cream, 35% fat
½ level teaspoon fleur de sel
8 egg yolks
80g caster sugar

1 SCRAPE OUT THE VANILLA POD
Split 1 vanilla pod in two and scrape it out with the blade of a knife to reserve the seeds.

2 HEAT THE MILK AND CREAM
Pour the semi-skimmed milk and cream into a saucepan. Add the vanilla pod with the seeds together with ½ level teaspoon fleur de sel. Bring to the boil.

3 BEAT THE EGG YOLKS AND SUGAR
Meanwhile, combine 8 egg yolks and 80g caster sugar in a mixing bowl. Whisk until the mixture is thick and pale.

4 COMBINE THE TWO MIXTURES
When the milk and cream mixture comes to the boil, pour it over the whisked egg yolks a half or third at a time, whisking vigorously all the while.

5 HEAT THE CREAM
Return the mixture to the saucepan over a low to medium heat and stir with a wooden spatula in a figure of 8 until the cream coats the spatula.

PHILIPPE'S TIPS

ROAST NUTS

Spread out the nuts (hazelnuts, almonds, pine nuts, pistachios, etc) on the baking tray and roast them right through for 12 to 15 minutes at 150°C (gas mark 2).

PEEL AND SLICE A PINEAPPLE

Slice off the base and top of the pineapple using a large sharp knife. Stand the pineapple upright and remove the peel by cutting from top to bottom following the contour of the fruit. When the pineapple is peeled, lay it down and slice it fairly thinly, then use a pastry cutter to cut out the centre of each slice. You can also take out the centre of the whole pineapple. To do that, you should leave it upright after peeling and insert the knife into the fruit then cut around the heart. Remove the cylinder you cut out.

ZEST A CITRUS FRUIT

If you don't have a zester, use a peeler to remove the coloured part of the zest (avoiding the white pith). Then slice the zest you removed very thinly with a knife.

SEGMENT A CITRUS FRUIT

Cut the base and top off the fruit. Sit it on a flat surface on a chopping board then remove the peel from top to bottom following the contour of the fruit. The strips you remove will reveal the flesh. Now pick up the fruit in your hand and, holding it over a dish to catch the juice, insert the blade of the knife between the segments of the fruit and remove them one by one.

PEEL A MANGO

You can peel a mango using an Econome knife then cut it into slices by slicing around the stone. But you can also cut the flesh into cubes by halving the mango: slice along the stone, remove the stone and cut a lattice shape into the flesh of each shell. Then, turn the shells inside out the way you would a sock, so that the mango cubes are pushed out and can easily be collected.

PREPARE CANDIED PEEL

It's best to blanch the zests before caramlising them. To do that, put the zests into a saucepan, cover with cold water and bring to the boil. Take off the heat, tip them into a sieve and reserve the peel. Repeat the process twice more.

Now return the blanched peel to the saucepan with the water and sugar and cook until candied for 40 minutes over a low heat.

PREPARE CANDIED GINGER

Peel 100g of fresh ginger, cut it into pieces and soak for 30 minutes in cold water. Drain, tip the pieces of ginger into a saucepan, cover with cold water and bring to the boil. Take off the heat, drain and put the ginger back in the saucepan. Cover with cold water, bring to the boil, drain and repeat the process once or twice more.

The last time, put the pieces of ginger into a saucepan with 600g of sugar and 1 litre of water. Bring to the boil then cook over a low heat until all the water has evaporated. The ginger should turn transparent. If that hasn't happened, add a bit of water and continue cooking.

PREPARE BEURRE MANIÉ (KNEADED BUTTER)

Put 600g softened butter (make sure you leave it out at room temperature for 30 minutes first) in the bowl of an electric mixer fitted with the paddle attachment. Add 200g flour and knead at low speed for 2 minutes. Regularly scrape around the sides of the bowl with a spatula to draw the mixture into the middle of the bowl. Continue kneading and increase the speed to medium. Count two minutes until the paste is firm and homogenous but still pliable. Take out the kneaded butter and place it between two sheets of baking parchment. Roll it out into a rectangle with 25 x 45cm sides. Refrigerate for 2 hours.

MELT BUTTER

Cut the butter into pieces. Put them in a saucepan and melt over a low heat. When half the butter has melted, remove from the heat and stir well until the butter is completely liquefied.

BLIND BAKE PASTRY

Baking blind means baking the pastry without a filling. To do that, line a flan tin with pastry, lay a sheet of baking parchment over the pastry and cover with a layer of dry pulses (beans, lentils, etc), then put it in the oven for the time indicated. You can also use silicone baking beans instead of dry pulses, which you can then re-use.

LINE A FLAN TIN

Roll out the pastry to about 5mm thick, then use the rolling pin to lay the pastry over the buttered and floured baking ring or flan tin. Proceed very carefully and allow the pastry to overhang the edges. Use the thumb of your left hand and the crooked first finger of your right hand to press the pastry carefully into the edges of the tin. Roll the rolling pin over the tin to eliminate the surplus pastry.

MELT CHOCOLATE

Break up the chocolate into a Pyrex® bowl. Place the bowl in a saucepan filled with water (the bottom of the bowl should not be touching the bottom of the pan) and set the pan over a medium heat. When half the chocolate has melted, take off the heat and stir well to obtain a smooth, homogenous mixture.

MAKE A GANACHE

Although proportions may vary according to the recipe and texture required, you can start from a basis of 40% chocolate for 60% milk or cream. The technique consists of boiling the cream (or milk) and pouring it over the pieces of dark chocolate in three batches, then whisking to create an emulsion.

MAKE CHANTILLY CREAM

Begin by making sure the cream (which needs to be at least 35% fat), the bowl and the whisk (or the accessories of the electric mixer) are cold. To do that, put them in the fridge for an hour or in the freezer for 15 minutes. It's also best to whip up the cream in a cool place. My personal advice is to place a smaller bowl in a bigger mixing bowl filled with ice cubes.

As you proceed, make sure you tilt the bowl and whisk from top to bottom always in the same way, evenly and without going too fast or too slowly. For sweetened cream, and contrary to what you may read here and there, you can incorporate the sugar at any point: it makes no difference whether you start or finish by adding it.

MAKE CARAMEL

How often do I hear: 'My caramel won't work out!' Yet there's nothing more simple. There are two ways of making caramel: you can boil the sugar with water or you can make it dry, just with sugar. For the dry method, simply heat the sugar over a low heat to the required caramel colour.

To make caramel using water, combine the sugar with 10% of its weight in water (e.g., 10ml water for 100g sugar). Stir well and cook over a low heat. Make sure you have a glass of cold water to hand to dip a pastry brush in and remove the sugar crystals from the sides of the pan. Otherwise, they are liable to fall in and agitate the caramel or make it lumpy.

Then just cook to the required caramel colour, bearing in mind that the lighter the caramel, the sweeter it will be, but that if it is too dark, it will be bitter. The ideal is a dark copper colour (which occurs at about 175°C to 176°C), when it is neither too sweet not too bitter.

To stop the caramel cooking, take it off the heat and sit the saucepan in a receptacle filled with iced water.

WHISK EGG WHITES TO PEAKS

Egg whites consist of water and albumen. The principle of whisking up egg whites is to incorporate air, exactly as you do for chantilly cream, for example. How stiff you make them depends on the recipe you are following. So, the whites will be more or less firm according to whether you are making a sponge or floating islands.

Start the process by breaking the eggs delicately to avoid any yolk disturbing the whites, because the smallest drop can stop the whites frothing up. You also need your whisk to be completely dry: if you rinse if off first, make sure you dry it thoroughly.

Also important is the freshness of the eggs. For a sponge mixture, floating islands or a chocolate mousse, use very fresh eggs. For macarons, however, I suggest taking 'old egg whites' that have aged for 3 or 4 days, because they will form peaks more easily.

Start by whisking the egg whites gently in a mixing bowl for 1 to 2 minutes to break them up. Then gradually increase the speed until the whites are frothy. To avoid them sinking, you should add the sugar (if the recipe involves sugar) at the start of the process.

For a meringue, the peaks should not be too stiff. If you are cooking them, cook at a low temperature: in a bain-marie if they are going in the oven, or in a very gently simmering liquid if you are cooking them in a saucepan.

If you are adding beaten egg whites to another mixture (melted chocolate or a mousse, for example), incorporate them half at a time: begin by adding 20 to 30% of the whisked egg whites, whisk vigorously to thoroughly combine and give body to the mixture, then carefully fold in the rest with a spatula, stirring from top to bottom and rotating the bowl.

RECIPE INDEX

A

Apple and Honey Spread	page 40
Apple Tartlets	page 136

B

Banana and Coffee Tart	page 146
Bittersweet Orange Cake	page 60
Blueberry and Almond Tart	page 148
Brioche Mousseline	page 30
Brown Sugar Waffles	page 74

C

Caramalised Ground Mixed Nuts	page 215
Caramel and Crystallised Ginger Tuiles	page 92
Caramels with Salted Butter	page 176
Chaussons Napolitains	page 28
Cherry Clafoutis	page 126
Chocolate Gâteau	page 122
Chocolate Mousse	page 76
Chocolate Sponge Cake	page 52
Citrus Fruit Jellies	page 190
Citrus Salad with a Tangy Jus	page 80
Coconut Snaps	page 104
Coconut, Ginger and Crunchy Sugar Cake	page 56
Coffee Cake	page 160
Conversation… Lemon and Hazelnut	page 58
Creamed Rice	page 68
Crème Anglaise	page 217
Crème Caramel	page 72
Crème Pralinée	page 216
Croissants	page 32

D

Dreamy Madeleines	page 54

F

Floating Islands, Vanilla and Praline	page 70
French Flan Pastry (pâte à foncer) in the electric mixer	page 214
Fruit Tagine	page 84
Fruit Tagine	page 213

G

Gâteaux Bretons with Brown Sugar	page 62
Goats Cheese Tart with Mango and Avocado	page 158
Gourmet Pains au Chocolat	page 26

H

Hazelnut and Fleur de Sel Streusel	page 180
Hazelnut and Fleur de Sel Streusel	page 212

L

Ladyfingers with Matcha Tea	page 106
Langues de Chat with Green Tea and White Chocolate	page 98

Lemon Cream Choux Buns   *page 164*
Light Kouign-amann   *page 24*

M
*t*Mango and Pineapple Tart   *page 140*
Marbled Chocolate and Hazelnut Cake   *page 48*
Marbled Praline Ice Cream   *page 188*

N
Nougat   *page 184*

O
Orange Tart   *page 144*

P
Paris-Brest   *page 118*
Pâte sucrée   *page 208*
Pear Tart with Champomy® Caramel   *page 142*
Praline Paste   *page 172*
Praline Shortbread   *page 94*
Puff Pastry in the electric mixer   *page 209*

Q
Quince Tarte Tatin   *page 138*

R
Raspberry and Matcha Tea Cake   *page 162*
Red Fruit Compote   *page 186*
Religious Dreams   *page 114*
Rhubarb Paste   *page 174*
Rhubarb Tart   *page 132*

Rich Coffee Log   *page 166*
Rum Babas   *page 120*

S
Saint-Honoré   *page 112*
Salambos   *page 124*
Semolina Cake   *page 82*
Snow Meringues   *page 156*
Soft Cantuccini   *page 96*
Spicy Almond and Fruit Fondant Biscuits   *page 90*
Spicy Banana Tuiles with Black Sesame Seeds   *page 100*
Sugared Almond Cake   *page 154*
Sweet Chocolate Ice Cream   *page 182*
Sweet Choux Pastry in the electric mixer   *page 210*

T
Tangy Strawberry Tart   *page 134*
Tangy Windmills   *page 34*
Tarte Tatin   *page 116*
Tasty Shortbread   *page 102*

V
Vanilla and Bergamot Follies   *page 36*
Vanilla and Sultana Briochins   *page 38*
Vanilla Crème Pâtissière   *page 178*
Vanilla Crème Pâtissière   *page 211*
Vanilla Flan   *page 50*

W
White Chocolate Lava Cakes with Lemon   *page 78*

ADDRESSES

LA PÂTISSERIE DES RÊVES
93, rue du Bac
75007 PARIS
Telephone : +33 (0)1 42 84 00 82

LA PÂTISSERIE DES RÊVES
111, rue de Longchamp
75016 PARIS
Telephone : +33 (0)1 47 04 00 24

LA PÂTISSERIE DES RÊVES
43 Marylebone High Street
London W1U 5HE
Telephone: 020 3603 7333
Twitter: @LPDR_London

LA PÂTISSERIE DES RÊVES
8-7 Kakuda-cho, Kita-ku, Underground (B1F)
Hankyu Umeda Store,
Osaka
Japan
Telephone: 06-6361-1381

LA PÂTISSERIE DES RÊVES
518 Washio-cho, Kodaiji-michi, Higashiyama-ku,
Kyoto
Japan
Telephone : +81 (0) 75 533 7041

LE SALON DE THÉ
111, rue de Longchamp
75016 PARIS
Telephone : +33 (0)1 47 04 00 24